the Cantonists
The Jewish Children's Army of the Tsar

LARRY DOMNITCH

Jerusalem

DEVORA
PUBLISHING

New York

THE CANTONISTS
The Jewish Children's Army of the Tsar

Published by DEVORA PUBLISHING COMPANY

Text Copyright © 2003 by Larry Domnitch
Cover and Book Design: David Yaphe
Editor: Fern Levitt

ISBN: 1-930143-79-6 (cloth)
ISBN: 1-930143-85-0 (paper)

Email: publisher@devorapublishing.com
Web Site: www.devorapublishing.com

Library of Congress Cataloging-in-Publication Data
Domnitch, Larry.
The cantonists: the Jewish children's army of the tsar / by Larry Domnitch.
   p. cm.
ISBN 1-930143-79-6 (Hardcover: alk. paper) — ISBN 1-930143-85-0 (Paperback: alk. paper)
1. Jews — Persecutions — Russia — History — 19th century.
2. Jewish soldiers — Russia — History — 19th century.
3. Jewish children — Government policy — Russia — History — 19th century.
4. Russia — Armed Forces — Recruiting, enlistment, etc. — History — 19th century.
5. Russia — Ethnic relations.

I. Title. DS135.R9D66 2004
355'.0089'924047—dc22
2003024194

Printed in Israel

Table of Contents

the Cantonists

The Jewish Children's Army of the Tsar

LARRY DOMNITCH

Preface

J ewish children, abducted from their families, struggling for survival and to preserve their Jewish identity in the face of the overwhelming pressure being applied by the Tsar's army — this is the saga of the Cantonists.

We have all heard echoes and whispers of this story. They have come down to us as part of the folklore of the Jewish people: how parents had their sons' fingers amputated or legs broken to avoid the draft, how families were betrayed by people they trusted, how sons were lost to their families and communities. Many of our own forebears left their families and emigrated from the Pale of Settlement precisely to avoid draft into the Tsar's army. Even years after the Cantonist epoch had ended, in the aftermath of the assassination of Tsar Alexander II in 1881, many Jews opted to emigrate out of fear that the Cantonist system would be reinstated. It was a terrifying episode in Jewish history, and one that is etched in the collective memory of the Jewish people. It was terrifying to those who escaped it, but even more so to the Cantonists themselves, the unfortunate and unwilling conscripts. Unable to escape the draft, many spent the major part of their lives in the Tsar's army.

Thousands of today's Jews are descendants of the Cantonists. In the century-and-a-half that have passed since the Cantonist era, two once-mighty Russian empires have fallen. Yet, descendants of many of the Cantonists who survived and maintained their Jewish identity continue to carry on the Jewish tradition of their forebears. The eternal legacy of the Jewish people lives on.

In the hidden back corners of libraries in Jerusalem, New York, and

Florida, I scoured sources on the history of Russian Jewry looking for information on the Cantonists. I found accounts in Hebrew, Yiddish and Russian. Rabbis of the era as well as *maskilim* (writers of the Jewish Enlightenment movement) wrote Hebrew accounts, often published in books and novels, of what they witnessed. The Yiddish materials included stories about the Cantonists written by Yiddish writers and numerous historical accounts published in history books based on the content of archives that became available in the years immediately prior to and following the Russian Revolution. The main Russian resource for this book, the journal *Yevreiskaya Starina*, contained many first-hand accounts of survivors as related in their old age for posterity. I am indebted to friends in the Russian-Jewish immigrant community who assisted me with translating these writings.

This volume is an attempt to collect a comprehensive anthology of these first-hand accounts of the era as recorded by Cantonists themselves and by eyewitnesses to their plight, and to make them accessible to English-speaking readers.

The stories paint a vivid picture of the events of this period. Each story is unique, though the stories share an undercurrent of human and Jewish suffering. The accounts have been translated from their original Russian, Yiddish, and Hebrew, excerpted, and adapted into narrative form.

The first chapter of this book sketches the historical context of the Cantonist phenomenon. Several chapters of short accounts follow, arranged thematically. The second half of the book contains lengthier accounts of individuals, each comprising its own chapter.

Former Cantonist Berke Finklestein wrote, years later, "These things may not be forgotten. We must tell them to our children and grandchildren."[1]

The stories are not easy reading, but they will further our insight into this dark period and honor the memories of the Jews and their families who suffered through it. It is my hope that the stories of those who suffered will be heard and remembered. *Y'hi zichram baruch* — May their memories be blessed.

Larry Domnitch
Denver, October 2003

The Arrival of the Storm: "The Jewish Problem"

As long as there have been Jews in Russia, anti-Semitism has been an integral thread of the fabric of Russian society.

When Tsarina Elizabeth Petrovna (1741–1761) came to the throne, Jews had been officially prohibited from living in Russia since the end of the fifteenth century. Over time, the exclusion laws had been relaxed for economic reasons. Jews had trickled back into Russia and re-established communities.

In 1742, Tsarina Elizabeth issued an expulsion decree calling for immediate deportation of all Jews from the Russian provinces. When members of the Russian Senate attempted to persuade her to cancel the decree, citing damage to the economy from the loss of the economic benefit Jews provided, the Tsarina replied, "I do not want to benefit from the enemies of Christ."[2]

Elizabeth Petrovna's decree permitted Jews to remain in Russia only if they accepted the tenets of the Russian Orthodox Church. However, this effort to induce the Jews to abandon their faith was futile. The decree did not persuade a single Jew to convert.[3]

When Poland collapsed thirty years later, in 1772, its territory was divided among Prussia, Austria and Russia. A partition treaty was signed that summer in the city of St. Petersburg. In this agreement, Russia received the adjacent provinces of Vitebsk, Polock, and Mohyev with their tens of thousands of Jewish inhabitants. This territorial acquisition presented a quandary: how should Tsarina Catherine, whose policy opposed Jewish settlement in her empire, handle the demographic

9

aspects of the new territories?

The Prussian and Russian invasion of Poland in 1782 led to another partition. In 1793, the Russians took much of the Ukraine and most of Belarus. A third partition in 1795 followed the failed revolt led by the Polish patriot Tadeusz Kosciuszko (1746–1817) and expanded Russian territory in Lithuania. This included the cities of Vilna and Grodno and the remaining sections of Belarus.

Russia's incremental acquisition of a Jewish population of several hundred thousand presented the Russians with a dilemma. They called it the "Jewish Problem." The very presence of Jews challenged the authority of the monarchy, which envisioned a unified kingdom of all nationalities, blending into a single people based on a common language and culture. The Jews had distinct traditions and resisted assimilation into Russian society, preferring to continue their community life in small villages. The solution chosen by the Russian leadership was to force Jews to assimilate or convert, or to make life so difficult that they would seek to emigrate.

Following the first partition, the Tsarina Catherine II initially issued a manifesto welcoming all new inhabitants. This manifesto did not exclude Jews. Catherine was not adverse to the notion of tolerance and to granting increased freedoms to the Jews. She, like her predecessors, had advisors who recognized the positive implications for the economy that resulted from more tolerant policies. However, the Russian people at large were of a different mind. Popular opinion decidedly opposed all such notions, and the Russian people consistently blamed the ills and misfortunes of Russia on the Jews. This soon forced the Tsarina to retreat from her tolerant position, resulting in the enactment of legislation that singled out the Jews for harsh treatment.

Catherine chose to act upon the allegations of merchants in Moscow when they complained in 1790 that Jewish merchants were undercutting local trade by selling foreign goods at discounted prices. In 1791, she authorized the first of the statutes that led to the definition of the area known as the "Pale of Settlement." These laws limited Jews to living only in those territories annexed from Poland. The Pale of Settlement restrictions were in force for well over a century, confining the Jews to the region between the Black Sea and the Baltic Sea and thereby limiting their mobility and economic opportunities.

Tsar Alexander Pavlovich I (1801–1825), like Catherine, was initially receptive to the notion of tolerance but did not attempt to implement such reforms given the opposition to them in Russian society. Alexander adopted a policy toward the Jews of "forceful encouragement" to accept baptism. During his reign, ever more aggressive measures were adopted to achieve large-scale conversion of the Jews.

On December 9, 1804, Alexander issued a "Statute Concerning Jews" which sought to compel Jewish assimilation into Russian society. Among its many provisions, the Statute called for the expulsion of Jews from small villages to larger towns and the weakening of the small-town economy. Alexander and his advisors evidently assumed that once they left their isolated environment, Jews would melt into society at large.

The various provisions of the statute attacked the "Jewish problem" from different angles with the ultimate intention of wearing down the Jews' resistance to accepting baptism. Laws prohibiting leasing of property and the sale of alcohol to peasants increased economic pressure. The Jews were authorized to establish schools with a general curriculum of secular studies, but these could be taught only in Polish, Russian, or German; it was forbidden to teach in Yiddish, the traditional vernacular of Eastern European Jewry. The law also restricted elected members of the *Kahal* (the government-authorized Jewish community council) to terms of three years. This measure was intended to weaken community leadership by limiting its influence and control.

Soon after the statute's enactment, expulsions began. The economic condition of the Jewish masses deteriorated from poverty to indigence. Thousands lost their livelihoods and relied on the funds of the Kahal.

In a further attempt to proselytize the Jews, Alexander created the "Society of Israelite Christians" on March 25, 1817. This organization proposed to shelter any Jews who would be shunned by the Jewish community for accepting Christianity. Converts were promised attractive benefits: property grants, the freedom to live anywhere in the Russian Empire, full civil equality, increased self-government, and a reduction of taxes. The anticipated groups of converts were to be managed by a special committee under the Tsar's supervision. Despite the widespread poverty and hardship within the Pale of Settlement, no Jews accepted the Tsar's offers.

Undeterred, the government persisted in its efforts to identify the inducement that would break the resistance of the Jews. In 1819, a large tract of land in the territory of Yekaterinoslav was set aside for future resettlement of the "Israelite Christians." This project also failed to attract any takers. The land sat empty.

Though the Jews were forced to relocate to large towns, they maintained cohesive Jewish communities. In 1822, Alexander passed further legislation offering yet greater inducements to Jews who renounced their Judaism. Even these promises of new freedoms and government support for land purchases elicited no interest from the Jewish community.

Alexander's intensified efforts to solve the "Jewish Problem" had failed miserably. The Jews stubbornly continued to live in poverty in their towns and cities, preferring this to the abandonment of their identity.

In 1825, an unfortunate twist of fate brought Nicholas Pavlovich (1825–1855) to the throne. When his oldest brother Tsar Alexander died, next in the line of succession was brother Constantine. Constantine, who was commander-in-chief of the Polish army, refused the throne; Nicholas ascended to the throne in his stead.

Nicholas held an uncompromising vision of a homogeneous Russian nation and displayed no tolerance for differing views and beliefs. He desired all the peoples of Russia to meld under the banner of the Russian Orthodox Church. Any expression of nonconformity was regarded as treason.

From the onset, Nicholas's rise to power worsened the circumstances of Russia's Jews. Nicholas was an anti-Semite who had for years expressed anti-Jewish views. In 1816, at age sixteen, Nicholas wrote in his diary, "The ruination of the peasants of these provinces is the *Zhids* (derogatory term for Jews). They are regular leeches and suck these unfortunate governments to the point of exhaustion. It is a matter of surprise that in 1812 they displayed exemplary loyalty to us and assisted us wherever they could at the risk of their lives."[4]

Nicholas regarded the Jews as an "injurious element" having no place in the Russian Empire. He advocated the abolition of Jewish autonomy and the complete assimilation of Russian Jewry. Aware of the failure of his predecessors to make headway on this point, Nicholas sought more stringent measures. It was his personal view that the Jews must be "corrected" by stern tutelage and discipline. Over his thirty-year reign, Tsar Nicholas enacted hundreds of anti-Jewish measures. For this reason, he was known by the Jews as "Haman the Second."

One measure adopted by Tsar Nicholas against the Jews of the Pale of Settlement towered above all others in its cruelty. In 1826, Nicholas instructed his ministers to draft a special Statute of Military Service imposing the draft on the Jews. He disregarded those of his advisors who warned that the decree was too harsh and would prove counterproductive. The young monarch's goal in imposing the draft was to weaken the Jews' cohesiveness and force them to accept Christianity. He evidently believed that since the obstinate older Jewish population would not voluntarily accept baptism, he would target the very young and use every available means to persuade them to do so. He devised a plan to separate the young by force from the shelter of their homes and families, even before they reached army age, and thereby coerce them into accepting baptism.

On August 26, 1827, Nicholas published the edict known as the *rekrutshina* (Recruitment Decree) calling for conscription of Jewish boys between the ages of twelve and twenty-five. Conscripts under the age of eighteen were to live in preparatory institutions until they were old enough to formally join the army. The twenty-five years of army service required of these recruits were to be counted from age eighteen, even if they had already spent many years in military institutions before reaching that age.

The Recruitment Decree did not specify the quota of recruits. This was to be established yearly for each district.

The term *canton* was used to refer to the areas where military barracks were established.[5] The Cantonist system had originated in 1721 during the reign of Tsar Peter the Great, who set up schools to provide rigid military training to trainees as young as age seven. When the children reached the age of fourteen, they were assigned to various regiments. (Later, the official draft age was raised to eighteen.) At the end of a soldier's term of service, he usually was unable to provide for his family, as years of army service took a heavy physical toll. The army provided for the family, thus maintaining its dependence on the Tsar and ensuring that the next generation would be forced to serve in its turn.

The Jews were not the only ones who hated and feared the Cantonist system. Russian non-Jews also suffered from this institution that separated young men from their families and imposed upon them a grueling life in the military. According to M. A. Kretchmer in his memoirs about recruitment under Nicholas I, "The word 'Cantonist' was the equivalent of a swear word. To be a Cantonist, if it was not worse than being a convict, was in any case, considered to be no better."[6]

Nicholas strengthened the Cantonist system and used it to single out Jewish children for persecution, their baptism being a high priority to him. No other group or minority in Russia was expected to serve at such a young age, nor were other groups of recruits tormented in the same way. There are indications that Nicholas required a higher proportion of the Jewish population to serve than was required of other groups. Nicholas wrote in a confidential memorandum, "The chief benefit to be derived from the drafting of the Jews is the certainty that it will move them most effectively to change their religion."[7] Historian Simon Dubnov wrote, "The barrack was to serve as a school, or rather as a factory, for producing a new generation of de-Judaized Jews, who were completely Russified and, if possible, Christianized."[8]

Tsar Nicholas I was more ambitious than any other European monarch in his attempts to bring Jews to Christianity.[9] Publicly, he denied that such religious coercion was taking place, since such policies were officially forbidden in Russia, but there is abundant evidence that the policy was deliberate.

During the reign of Nicholas I, approximately seventy thousand Jews,[10] some fifty thousand of whom were children, were taken by force from their homes and families and inducted into the Russian army[11] where most served in non-combat roles. The boys, raised in the traditional Jewish community of the *shtetl* (Yiddish term for a small Jewish town), were pressured via every possible means, including torture, to accept baptism. Many resisted, and some managed to maintain their Jewish identity. The magnitude of their struggle is difficult to conceive.

This thirty-year period saw the Jewish community in an unrelieved state of panic. Parents lived in perpetual fear that their children would be the next to fill the Tsar's quota. A child could be snatched away from any place at any time. Every moment might be the last spent together; when a child left for *cheder* (Jewish religious school) in the morning, parents could not know whether they would ever see him again. When they retired after singing him to sleep, they never knew whether they would have to struggle with *chappers* (kidnapper, chap is the Yiddish term for grab) during the night in a last-ditch attempt to hold onto their son. For this reason, rabbi, historian and author Yaakov Lipshitz referred to this era as "the sea of tears."[12]

The famed writer and folk poet Eliyakum Zunser, himself a Cantonist, compared the suffering of the Cantonists to the suffering of Jewish children in other eras of Jewish history. "The mothers who were robbed of their children by the Egyptians, the Romans and the Spanish priests had, at least, the sad comfort of knowing that their little ones were spared from long and great sufferings — by a quick death. The bereaved mothers in the days of Nicholas I had not even that much 'comfort.' Their young were snatched away from them, scattered in the faraway snow fields of Siberia, or in the steppes of the Caucasus."[13]

The Jewish community immediately grasped the implications of the Recruitment Decree. Synagogues were filled with petitioners beseeching God's mercy. Some tried to petition the government.

Legendary stories have come down to us of the many measures taken by young men and their families in their attempts to avoid the draft. They hid in the woods,[14] escaped to another province, or traveled abroad. Some lived as vagrants, concealing their identities, hiding in the streets and back alleys of Jewish neighborhoods. Many children were smuggled to Poland, where the conscription of Jews did not take effect until 1844. Mothers hid their children in cellars. Often, parents avoided reporting the birth of an infant to the government so that there would be no official record in the population registry of his existence. Boys were dressed in girls' clothing and braids and taught to speak as girls. Those with adequate funds attempted to bribe officials. Poor families begged to obtain money with which to redeem their children from army duty.

Initially, there were a number of categories of exemption from the draft, and every potential exemption was exploited to its fullest. In fact, in some places the Jews were so resourceful that there was not a single person left eligible for the draft.[15] Since invalids were exempt from conscription, mothers had "surgeons" cripple children by breaking their arms or legs; some mutilated themselves by cutting off a finger or having an eye removed.[16] The exemption for married men led to marriages between young children.[17] Enrollment in yeshivas significantly increased, since yeshiva students were exempt. Others joined the lowest rank of the privileged merchants' guilds, artisan trade unions, or the ranks of factory mechanics, which were all exempt. Though they might in actuality have had no trade, they somehow managed to pay their dues and taxes, thereby maintaining their exempt status.

Though a significant proportion of eligible young men found ways to avoid the draft, government quotas of recruits remained in force. It was the duty of the Kahal[18] to ensure that the quotas were met. The Kahal was thus under tremendous pressure and had a serious moral dilemma. If they did not provide recruits to fill the quota, the government would punish the Jewish communities with more severe measures, such as increasing the quota of recruits. What was the least damaging way to meet their community's quota? Should they force young married men, still in their teens and already supporting a wife and children, into the army?

Faced with this agonizing decision, the Kahal often chose to conscript the very young on the basis that they did not yet have dependents. Needless to say, this policy did not provide a trivial solution, since no family would volunteer its child for the draft. The Kahal, therefore, resorted to the infamous institution of the chapper. The Kahal paid a fee to a chapper for each child he abducted and turned over to the army toward fulfillment of the community's quota. Jewish chappers, familiar with the community's language and habits, proved most effective in locating and abducting these children.[19]

To the unscrupulous chappers, the abduction of children was a profitable business. Some chappers stayed in their own districts, while others traveled throughout the Pale from town to town. Once chappers had caught a child, they held him captive until he could be turned over to the authorities for induction. *Dilaturia* (paid informers) often assisted the chappers in locating children.[20]

There were severe repercussions for those who defied the government. If the quotas were not met, the government could demand even more recruits. For example, in 1850, the Jews of Berditchev fell short of their quota by forty-five recruits. In punishment, they had to supply three times as many recruits, none under the age of twenty, for a total of one hundred and thirty-five.[21]

Despite this enormous pressure from the government, the question remains: what drove so many Kahal leaders to cooperate with the authorities, resorting to such cruel measures as paying kidnappers to turn over children in order to satisfy the quota?

We can only speculate on the logic by which members of the Kahal rationalized their complicity with the authorities. Perhaps they viewed cooperation with the Tsar as the community's only viable option. Perhaps they concluded that resistance would be futile; as the Jews were at the mercy of the Tsar, it was presumably considered paramount not to provoke him in order to ensure the survival of the community as a whole. The Kahal leaders may even have seen the decree as a temporary crisis that would soon pass, not anticipating that it would continue for thirty long years.

For many members of the Kahal, selfish motives took precedence. Some Kahal leaders feared that failure to provide recruits would result in their own exile to Siberia. Others acted for personal gain, since the government paid a fee to the Kahal for each child abducted.

The records do tell of some Kahal leaders who defied the Tsar's orders and, at personal risk, either prevented the recruitment of Cantonists or attempted to reduce the quotas.[22] And while many members of the Kahal and the chappers they employed caused considerable damage to the Jewish community, they were, statistically, a small minority.

The vast majority of Jews abhorred these practices, and the policies of the Kahal leadership drew sharp criticism from within the Jewish community. Rabbi Baruch HaLevi Epstein, a nineteenth century rabbinic luminary,[23] called the era "the sins of the Kahal."[24] Rabbi Epstein wrote of the Kahal leaders, "This was an unprecedented time of trouble in

Jewish history, when the best of the people, whose job and responsibility was to supervise the welfare of the nation and to prevent injustice in the community, ruled and lowered themselves to doing wickedness to their brothers. And the animal-like cruel regime attacked, like lions and tigers, without any human feeling and with no mercy or justice. This was an era whose evil, wickedness, and cruelty reached until the furthest firmament. The land shook and the skies trembled, mountains and valleys cried, and rivers and streams were filled with tears."[25]

The Hebrew writer Yehudah Leib Levin wrote of the hypocrisy of the Kahal leadership, "The question depressed me to the point where I began to be afraid of Jews, of my Jewish brothers. One day I saw the head of the community; I was told he was the head of the Kahal and I was shocked. Did I not know him? Was he not steeped in Torah? Every Friday afternoon as he got out of the *mikva* [ritual bath] with the water still dripping from his *peyot* [side locks] he would pass through the market with his stick in his hand and shout: 'Women! Candle lighting!' And if the women shopkeepers did not hurry to close their shops, did he not oust them with his stick? And how honorable and pleasant it was to see a learned, eminent man, staying up the whole of Thursday night in the seminary, studying until the morning. He is elegant in the manner he dresses, and he warns others against the desecration of the Sabbath. Yet he is the very head of the Kahal! He is the governor and the commander, and at his command infants are plucked from their mother's laps, fathers are taken from their children, and he would go in person to seek out people without papers, to abduct them and deliver them to the army with his holy hands! I went crazy from what I saw."[26]

Eliyakum Zunser wrote of the Kahal officials, "Still greater, and yet more terrible, is the cruelty of these deputies at the military conscriptions. These 'excellent Jews' in their long coats, and the 'holy' skullcaps on their piously shaven heads, were transformed into ravaging, bloodthirsty beasts."[27]

Dividing the cohesive Jewish community and lowering its collective morale was no doubt one of the objectives of Nicholas's policy. Nothing had ever torn at the close-knit Jewish society of the Pale of Settlement like the Cantonist decree. The sacrifice of so many children by the Kahal, its kidnappers and informers left the families and friends of the tens of thousands of victims bitter and distraught.

The decree, in addition, pitted wealthy Jews against poor. According to the law, a Jewish family was allowed to substitute a "volunteer" recruit of the same age for its own child. Wealthy families bribed usually corrupt Kahal officials for draft exemptions for their own sons. In their stead, the Kahal turned in boys from poor families to fill the quota. A stanza from a popular Yiddish poem of the era expresses the bitterness this caused: "Rich Mr. Rockover has seven sons, not one a uniform dons. But poor widow Leah has only one child, and they hunt him down as if he were wild."[28]

In July 1853, on the pretext of needing more recruits to fight the Crimean War, Nicholas passed a new decree that tore the Jewish community further asunder. Any Jew caught without a valid passport was deemed a *piyamnike* (the old Russian/Polish term for "vagrant" that was applied to Jews caught without valid papers) and could be turned in at the army recruiting office. In return for such a recruit, the informer or the person who delivered the piyamnike would receive an exemption for a member of his own family.[29] Thus, any Jew found without the proper papers (which often happened when papers were confiscated or when they expired due to bureaucratic delays) could become the next victim at the hands of his fellow Jew. The new recruit's capture would secure the children of the one who handed him over. One never knew whether any stranger encountered had reason to turn *you* in.[30]

This decree was intended by Nicholas to serve as a three-year experiment, at the end of which time he would measure the increase in the recruitment resulting from providing incentives to individual Jews to save their own families by betraying each other. The offered reward had its desired effect. Toward the end of the Cantonist era, individual Jews turned in others to save members of their own families.

As a result of the Cantonist Recruitment Decree, the Jews of Russia would never again view each other in the same way. The unity of the Jewish community was dealt a deeply damaging blow, and, one might claim never fully recovered from the trauma of betrayal by fellow Jews.

Despite the bleakness of this picture, heroism often prevailed. The history of the Cantonist period includes moving accounts of immense courage. Many individuals resisted the influence of the Kahal and protected and rescued children at risk of conscription. The price paid by those who protected boys from the military was apparent, as the government threatened severe punishments for Jews who interfered with the recruitment process. On November 27, 1838, the Tsar approved a law stating: "Jews who incite their fellow Jews to escape military service or help them hide shall be turned in as recruits themselves by order of the Provincial Government." Those found assisting potential draftees to avoid the draft, even if they themselves were not fit for army service, could be sent to hard labor.[31] Despite such attempts to discourage rescue efforts, they continued unabated.

The historical record describes numerous instances of communities uniting to defy the Kahal and protect their children, regardless of the consequences. Revolts took place in cities such as Mirrer, Neizager, and Volhynia. Some groups, both of Mitnagdim (Jews of Lithuania who opposed many elements of Hasidic philosophy) of the Lithuanian yeshivas and of Hasidim, managed to organize themselves, evade the scrutiny of the Tsar's officials, and save children despite efforts of Kahal leaders to the contrary.

Many yeshiva heads and rabbinical leaders also resisted the policies of the Kahal. For example, Rabbi Aharon Isaac Epstein of Minsk granted permission to a mob to use whatever force was necessary to free captive children. The rabbi was tried for this act and had the good fortune of being acquitted. Rabbi Joseph Baer Soloveitchik from Slutsk once broke down a fence to rescue a boy. For this deed, he was driven out of town. Rabbi Samuel, a rabbinical court judge in Grodno, hid children destined for the draft in his home, protecting and feeding them. Such efforts spared thousands of boys from the Cantonist fate.

Finally, we come to the resistance of the children themselves. The Cantonists were widely regarded by the Jewish community as heroes for their self-sacrifice. This attitude is illustrated in many of the stories in the current volume. During a period when Jews in other parts of Europe were voluntarily undergoing baptism to gain an "admission ticket" to European society, the Cantonists, despite their youth, were demonstrating extraordinary tenacity and dedication to their heritage. As children were being torn away from their grief-stricken parents, the parents' parting words were often "Remain a Jew!" Multitudes of Cantonists struggled and gave their lives in their attempts to comply.

Child recruits faced harsh conditions and many died shortly after induction. Some recruits, adamant in their refusal to accept baptism, endured multifarious tortures over prolonged periods but eventually succumbed. Many submitted to the pressure and accepted baptism, but a considerable minority held out, maintained their Jewish identity, and physically survived their ordeal.

There are records of Cantonists who, though forced to accept baptism, inwardly maintained their Jewish convictions. Eventually, after completing their army service, they returned to the Jewish community. An example is the case of twenty soldiers stationed near the city of Vitebsk who announced, in 1852, that since they had been converted by force, they were leaving Russian Orthodoxy and returning to Judaism. Shortly after their announcement, the soldiers were transferred out of the area; Vitebsk is a city with a large Jewish community that evidently was thought by the authorities to exert an unsettling influence. The spirit of rededication to their heritage remained with this group of soldiers despite their transfer from the heavily Jewish city where they were stationed.[32]

Perhaps most remarkable are the accounts of Cantonists who, after years of service, had forgotten that they were even Jews. Somehow, a trigger event — usually renewed contact with other Jews — reminded them of their Jewish past and re-ignited a spark of Jewish feeling. Such was the case with Tuvia Silverman, whose story is told later in this book.

After their years of service to the Tsar, some Cantonists returned home and took up their lives. Others had forgotten the locations of their original homes and settled in central Russia instead. Some Cantonists were so accustomed to army life that they could not even fathom the notion of returning to the world of the shtetl. The accounts of the survivors, most of which were written years after their discharge, give testimony to the variety of tragic and remarkable stories.

The Cantonist era came to an end with the death of Tsar Nicholas on February 19, 1855. As one Cantonist memoir notes, this was, appropriately enough, the holiday of Purim.[33] Alexander II, Nicholas's son and successor, ascended the Russian throne and signed the treaty of Paris that ended the Crimean War. One of the very first edicts issued by Alexander II abolished the Cantonist Decree in the Manifesto of August 26, 1856. The manifesto forbade pressure on Cantonist soldiers to accept baptism and reduced the draft quotas for Jews to a proportion of the population equal to that required of non-Jews.

The abolition of the Cantonist institution was only the first reform of many enacted during the reign of Alexander II, as he recalled many of his father's other extreme edicts. Later that year, a decree reduced the term of army service for Cantonists to fifteen years. About three years later, on July 9, 1859, Alexander issued another decree returning those under the age of twenty to their parents and ordered that they be exempt from service until they had reached that age.

The traumatic era finally came to an end, but its impact and scars lingered and continue to affect the Jewish world up to the present day.

The Cantonists often sacrificed their lives or their Jewish identities in their struggles. Those who survived endured prolonged suffering, even more so to remain members of the Jewish community. The boys themselves are, no doubt, the great heroes of this story.

Abductions

Tears are pouring into the streets,
Bathed in children's blood,
Tiny chicks are torn from school,
And dressed in uniforms.
Alas, what bitterness. Will day ever dawn?
— *from an anonymous Yiddish poem*[34]

This chapter contains accounts of the kidnap and capture of recruits. The first half of the chapter describes the kidnapping of young children. The second half describes the period in which the net widened to trap *piyamnikes*, Jewish boys and men of any age who were branded as vagrants because, allegedly, they did not hold valid identity papers.

Child-Snatching

This account was recorded by the Hebrew writer, Yehudah Leib Levin, from the eyewitness who related it to him:

One afternoon, a cart pulled by two majestic horses drew up to a house. Six heavy-set men with thick red necks entered the house and soon emerged holding a six-year-old boy who was screaming and flailing his arms. They dragged him by the neck to their wagon. A wild-haired woman burst out of the house, screaming bitterly, "My child! My chick!" In desperation, she attempted to overcome the men. Two of the men fought her off, threw her to the ground and fled. Meanwhile, the other four men rushed the child onto the cart and held him there by the throat. Those who had fought with the woman caught up to the cart and jumped on

23

board as it rumbled away. The wounded mother lay in misery on the ground, banging her head on the cobblestones, pulling out her hair with a resounding and bitter cry: "My son! My chick! Oh me, my child!"[35]

A. S. Friedberg recounts an episode in which no one heard the cries of the kidnapped child nor those of his blind father:

An elderly blind man lived with his ten-year-old son. In his younger years, the old man had been the cantor and emissary of the town until he had contracted an eye disease and could no longer perform the functions of his job. He begged for bread to feed his family, his young son guiding him from town to town. As they walked through the forest one winter day, chappers abducted his son. Alone and lost in the forest, the blind cantor screamed for help until he lost his voice, but nobody heard the old man's cries. The next day, the cantor was found dead, frozen to death in the forest.[36]

Yehudah Leib Levin describes the parting words of parents to their sons:

Captured children were squeezed tightly together in the wagon that uprooted them without warning from their world of the shtetl. A large, wide wagon pulled by two horses would rumble through the streets of a small village one day. The wagon drivers advanced from house to house, seizing boys out of each house until the wagon was filled. The boys were sitting or lying pressed against one another like fish in a barrel. Their parents, relatives and neighbors crowded around the wagon, crying bitterly. Parents thrust into the hands of their sons books of Psalms, sets of *tefillin* (phylacteries), whatever small religious article they had in their possession. "Stay a Jew!" they entreat their boys. "Whatever happens, stay a Jew!"[37]

The following story shows how the system succeeded in pitting Jew against Jew:

In the city of Zhitomir, a poor Jewish woman went to the market on Friday to beg for food for the Sabbath. She carried a small infant in her arms and her ten-year old son walked by her side. The proprietor of a market stall asked her where she lived, and she told him that she was from the area of Kiev. He gave her a loaf of bread and told her that if she would wait, he would bring her candles for the Sabbath.

The shopkeeper signaled to his son to slip away and fetch the chappers, who then tore the boy away from his mother and carried him to the army headquarters. The tears and wails of the poor mother went unheeded. The "generous" man had protected a member of his own family at her expense.[38]

One may despise the mother in the following incident, but sympathize with her misfortune:

In the city of Berditchev, a peasant woman knocked on the door of the Jewish butcher's wife as she was working in her store. The peasant confided to her in a whisper that two Jewish boys who would eat only kosher food were hiding in her home. She requested some kosher provisions for them.

Now, this woman's husband was hiding their two children from the chappers but would not divulge their hiding place to her, since her desire to visit them in their hideout might lead to their discovery. Thus, the woman had no idea that these two boys were her own children. She saw the peasant's request as an opportunity to turn these boys in as substitutes for her own sons so that her own sons could safely come home.

The butcher's wife gave the peasant woman a good cut of meat and asked her where she lived, ostensibly so she could bring her more meat. In her innocence, the peasant woman revealed the location. The woman quickly closed up her shop and hurried to the synagogue. She went to the community room of the Kahal to inform the community elders of the boys' hiding place. She accompanied the Kahal representatives on the wagon that took them to the village of the peasant woman. There she sent the chappers ahead to extract the boys from their hiding place.

She was stunned when she realized that the captive youths were her own sons. Her horrified screams at what she had brought to pass fell upon deaf ears.[39]

A Tiny Recruit:

A new recruit from the town of Simiyatitz — a five-year-old boy wearing only his shirt and *tzitzit* (ritual fringes), both of which were too long for his short legs — was brought into the administrative office in the district capital. There he was inducted into the army.

A few days later, the "warrior" was seen in the streets of the town, wearing the uniform of the recruits. His reddish coat and beret were many sizes too large. All that could be seen of him, peeking out between his collar and his hat, was his tiny mouth. His little voice, shrill as a whistle, could be heard crying out, "My mother! My mother!"[40]

There are many stories of mothers who, in their agony, protested before the Kahal in the synagogue. Here is one:

In 1853, a poor widow whose son had been kidnapped by the chappers burst into the synagogue in Minsk. She declared that she would not permit anyone to remove the Torah scrolls from the ark until action had been taken to save her son. The *gabbai* (the synagogue official who assigns honorary functions during the service) and the Kahal leaders were startled at first by her brazen outburst. However, one of the leaders of the community soon put an end to the commotion. He called out arrogantly to the Kahal members, "What impudence, that some woman dares to disturb the prayer! Pay no attention to her, and take out the Torah scroll!" The sobbing mother was shoved aside, and they carried on with the service.

> The widow pushed her way back to the ark, and raising her eyes to heaven, she cried out, "*Riboyne Shel O'lem* (Master of the Universe), You take pride in our forefather Abraham, who consented to sacrifice his own son Isaac. Order me to kill my only son, and I will obey You. But You would never have gotten Abraham's consent to surrender his son for baptism..."[41]

This incident took place in a synagogue in Kovno, during the Sabbath morning service at which Rabbi Israel Salanter[42] was praying:

> A woman whose son had been abducted interrupted the Sabbath morning service just as the Torah was about to be removed from the ark. Some of the worshippers pushed her aside as she made her way towards the Holy Ark. Rabbi Salanter intervened and came to her aid. He rebuked those who acted with such callousness toward her. After the Torah was brought out, Rabbi Salanter left the synagogue and finished his prayers privately at home, stating that praying in the synagogue at that moment was prohibited.[43]

The Vulnerable Piyamnikes

In July 1853, a new law authorized Jews to detain "piyamnikes." The law offered rewards for the capture of piyamnikes, and many Jews complied by turning in other Jews. The purpose of this measure was supposedly to prevent the hiding of Jews from recruitment. In fact, it provided a simpler way for a Jewish community to meet its quota of recruits. Gangs of chappers entered towns to root out piyamnikes or lay in wait for travelers by the roadside.

The new law encouraged the unscrupulous to ensure that potential recruits would not be found to hold a passport that might interfere with their eligibility for conscription. Therefore, even valid papers usually offered little protection. The valid passports of recruits were often confiscated and destroyed. Jews whose passports were approaching expiration were commonly detained until their passports expired, then seized as vagrants. In many cases, valid passports were revoked under the pretext that the recorded description of the passport holder did not match the appearance of its bearer.

Many of the piyamnikes were impoverished Jews of Lithuania, traveling by wagon to other provinces in search of employment. To pay for the journey, a traveler would give the driver his passport as collateral and then, once he found a job, redeem it with his first earnings. Often, the drivers sold the passports before they could be redeemed.

Such abuses threatened most Jews who dared to travel. Only travelers with the good fortune to be too young or too old for conscription were allowed to pass unmolested. Some merchants paid an exorbitant ransom for their own release.

Here are some accounts of abductions of unfortunate piyamnikes.

Expired Passport

A Jew with an expired passport was traveling home with his wife and five children. They were detained in a certain village. Local chappers turned in the man and his oldest son, thereby filling their community's quota of recruits. The two next-oldest boys were sold to another community, which did the same. The poor mother and her remaining two children, too young for service, were deported to their home country.[44]

To Save Himself

A Jew named Yisroel Chovas who lived in Chutin was ordered to report to the military. In Chutin lived another Jew who came from Deretchin, named Ber Dembravoski. He had raised his nine-year-old nephew, an orphan named Avrum Pederov.

To save himself, Yisroel told the chappers that a small child was hiding at Dembravoski's home. The chappers went to the house and kidnapped the child when Dembravoski was not at home. The official excuse for the abduction was that the child had no passport.[45]

Outsmarting the Chappers

Chappers whose specialty was hunting Jews without passports came in the night from a neighboring district town to a certain Jew who lived at an isolated inn in the Podolsk province. The walls of the inn were not very solid, having been built of a mixture of clay and straw. The chappers easily broke through a wall and kidnapped the Jew's young son, planning to turn him in as a piyamnike.

When the father found out who had taken his son, he proposed to them that for fifty rubles, his son could be exchanged for another of his sons whom he loved less. They agreed to the deal and the substitution was made. However, when the kidnappers brought the "less favorite son" to the recruiting office, he turned out to be a girl dressed in boy's clothing.[46]

Happy Ending

On a snow-covered roadway at the exit from the recruiting office in a certain city, a desperate woman threw down the six-month-old baby in her arms and fell to her knees before the army recruiter. She and her two older children begged for mercy for their husband and father. He had come to the city office in order to obtain a passport and instead had been turned in as a recruit.

The merciful army recruiter ordered the man's release. Fortunately, this noble fellow held a different view of the matter from that of his colleagues.

Father and Son

In a small town, a young boy was caught, fettered like a calf, and shipped by wagon to the regional capital. The chappers took him as a substitute for a member of the family of a rich man whose patronage the community desired.

When the boy's father heard that his only son had been captured, he dropped everything and, coatless, dashed out of his tailor shop in pursuit of the wagon. Swift as a deer, he overtook the horses at some distance from the town, grabbed their reins to stop them and pulled his son away from the thugs.

However, in his haste to give chase to the chappers, the father had inadvertently crossed the town's borders without his travel pass. The chappers overpowered him and tied him up. They put him in stocks and took him, together with his son, to the regional capital.

29

Family Destroyed

Once, attorneys from one town came to another and grabbed a Jew who seemed to them a suitable recruit. The local community then seized the captured man's son as a piyamnike to fill its own quota.

When the Jew's daughter heard the news, she collapsed and died of anguish. The grief-stricken mother did not know what to do first: run after her husband, try to save her son, or bury her daughter.[47]

Betraying Relatives

In a certain town, the tax collector made a business out of trading Jews without passports. He had accumulated a considerable fortune. In his greed, he even sold his own two nephews.[48]

Childhood Transformed

They were beloved and pleasant in their lifetimes, and in their deaths are not parted (from Him). They were swifter then eagles and stronger then lions to do the will of their Possessor. And the desire of their Rock, our God, will remember them favorably.
— *from the Av HaRachamim prayer*

When the Recruitment Law of Nicholas was enacted, each community was given specific instructions as to its quota of recruits. Official draft notices were sent to the Jewish communities in sealed envelopes marked "Top Secret." Three messengers were sent to every community, since a lone messenger would have been easy to bribe into reducing the number of required recruits.[49]

The chappers took precautions that made escape extremely difficult. Every child seized was locked into a secure holding place with his feet chained until he was deported. Generally, they were held in the Kahal administration building. Sometimes, two recruits were chained together. Minimal contact was allowed between the captive child and his family in order to limit any further influence on the child by his family. Parents caught attempting to speak with their children often faced punishment.[50]

When a group of young captive recruits had been assembled, they would depart. If it was summer, the group traveled on foot. In the winter, they were transported by wagon.

The average Cantonist group contained two hundred and fifty boys. A full battalion was made up of four such groups. Each group had its own generals and officers.

This chapter contains accounts of the departure and subsequent journeys of the young Cantonists.

Departure

"Listen brothers," Michel the candle maker cried out years later, under the thrall of a flood of painful memories. "Whoever did not see them 'driving' Jewish boys that day, in a detachment of four hundred, has not seen the light of God.... There they are, little and sickly, in long soldiers' overcoats hanging loose, an *arshin* (one arshin equals twenty-eight inches) longer than their legs, in tall caps pulled down to their eyes. The instructors are urging them on with punches and slaps.... This happened on a Friday, just before the lighting of the Sabbath candles. The people are drowning in tears, sobbing violently, as though for the destruction of the Temple. Their cries are so strong that they could cause the dead to rise from the grave!.... Our rabbi walks outside the town, stands on a table and tries to comfort them as they pass, and exhorts them to remain Jews despite the suffering at hand. A groan is just a groan!...."[51]

Haunting Memories

I happened upon some fellows with the backs of their heads shaven in the style of young recruits, running from an office, almost naked. I saw the tears and heard the sobbing of the mothers of these poor wretches whose heads had been shaved as a mark of their fitness to serve....

I recall seeing a whole line of carts, each full of little Jewish children piled together in the same way they haul calves to Petersburg. They were being taken under escort to a place where they would be brought into the Orthodox faith as Cantonist soldiers. Their sad faces still live in my memory.[52]

Long March

In 1835, the Russian revolutionary and writer Alexander Herzen, in exile in the city of Viatka near Perm, Siberia, encountered a group of new recruits. They were falling into line to continue their long march toward the Siberian city of Kazan. Herzen asked their officer about the children. This is what he recorded:

> "Oh, don't ask; it would break your heart. Well, I suppose my superiors know all about it; it is our duty to carry out orders and we are not in charge, but looking at it as a human being, it is an ugly business."

"Why, what is it?"

"You see, they have collected a crowd of cursed little Jew boys of eight or nine years old. Whether they are taking them for the navy or what, I don't know . At first, the orders were to drive them to Perm. Then there was a change, and we are driving them to Kazan. It took them over a hundred *versts* [about sixty miles] out of their way back there. The officer who handed them over said, 'It's dreadful, and that's all there is to it; a third were left on the way,' and he pointed to the earth. 'Not half will reach their destination,' he said."

"Have there been epidemics?" I asked, deeply moved.

"No, they just die off like flies. A Jew boy, you know, is such a frail, weak creature, like a skinned cat. He is not used to marching through the mud for ten hours a day and eating only biscuits — what's more, being among strangers, no father nor mother nor petting; well, they cough and cough until they cough themselves into their graves. And I ask you, what use is it to the army? What can they do with little boys?"

I did not respond.

They rounded up the children and formed them into regular ranks; it was one of the most awful sights I have ever seen. Those poor, poor children! Boys of twelve or thirteen might somehow have survived it, but little fellows of eight and ten.... Not even a brush full of black paint could capture such horror on canvas.

Pale, exhausted, with frightened faces, weighted down by their thick, clumsy soldiers' overcoats with stand-up collars, they fixed helpless pathetic eyes on the garrison soldiers who were pushing them roughly into ranks. The white lips, the blue rings under their eyes bore witness to fever or chill. These sick children, without care or kindness, exposed to the raw wind that blows unobstructed from the Arctic Ocean, were going to their graves.[53]

Torture and Baptism

After an agonizing journey, lasting as long as a year, the surviving children arrived at their destination emaciated, weak, and traumatized. Groups of one to two hundred children usually arrived two or three times a year. The commander of the base would send a contingent of soldiers to meet the new arrivals. The boys were brought into a bare, unheated room without even straw on the floor. Any possessions the children had managed to hold on to through the journey, including tzitzit, *siddurim* (prayer books), and tefillin, were confiscated. They were made to sit on the cold floor, where they sat weeping, frozen, with teeth chattering throughout the night. In the morning, the commander arrived bringing food but also wielding a whip.

The effort to break the children's will and prevail on them to accept baptism commenced immediately upon their arrival. The recruits were allowed no contact with other Jews. They were kept in a military establishment separate from adult Jewish recruits who might otherwise have encouraged them to resist. Some were kept in jails or placed in Christian homes under the care of a *diadke* (Russian for "uncle," implying a protector who ushers the boys into their new faith).[54]

After their release from jail or the diadkes' homes, when the recruits approached their battalions, the army again sent out soldiers to meet them. These officers once more tried to convince them to accept baptism.[55]

Priests who were promised rewards for persuading boys to accept baptism engaged in constant proselytizing. They often transferred the more resistant boys to other battalions away from boys they believed to be more impressionable. The priests conversed privately with the Cantonists, hoping to circumvent the effects of peer pressure to resist conversion. Officers in the battalions of boys who had been transferred for persistent stubbornness took a tougher approach.[56]

The proselytizers soon discovered that many of the boys were well-versed in Judaism and able to hold their own in theological debates. They also discovered that many were determined to honor their parents' parting request to remain steadfast in their faith. One missionary complained in a letter in 1844 that, when he spoke with the Jewish Cantonists, they responded with unyielding proofs for why they must remain Jews. He wrote, "It is very difficult for the priests to disprove these arguments; they don't have enough books."[57]

The recruits were required to attend church regularly. The church ceremonies were performed with exaggerated enthusiasm to strengthen their attraction for the young soldiers. In addition to the standard ceremonies, special prayers were added in the morning and evening, before and after eating, and before military drills in order to immerse the boys in ritual throughout the day.[58] Such "temptation" usually had little or no impact. The overwhelming majority of boys remained resolute. Conversion efforts could not simply overturn years of Jewish education.

When "friendly" persuasion failed, the Cantonists were often threatened with violence and torture if they did not accept baptism.[59] Those who still refused were tortured. Some accepted baptism out of fear of torture. Many others resisted even these threats.

In one such instance, a Cantonist boy was issued his official allotment of clothing for the year and ordered to store it in his trunk. When he looked for his clothes in the morning he discovered that they were missing. His immediate superior, a lance corporal or squad leader, rushed over and described to the trembling boy the horrors that awaited a hapless Cantonist for the "squandering" of official belongings, including birching and running the gauntlet. The boy cried bitterly and begged his superior to save him from punishment. "Be baptized," advised his mentor, "and the brass will forgive you."

In another reported instance, a commander asked some soldiers, "Who are these boys?" The soldiers replied, "These are Jews." The commander said, "Bring knives and axes. I will kill them all. I don't need *Zhids* (derogatory term for Jews). I will throw them into the fire. The Zhids killed our savior. They are cursed."

The children heard this exchange and were terrified. The commander called to one of the frightened boys, "Come here! Who are you?" The child identified himself, to which the commander replied, "Do you want to be baptized? If you cooperate, you will enjoy a warm meal. If you refuse, I will beat you to death."[60]

When threats of violence failed to convince the Cantonists to convert, every potential opportunity for torture was exploited. No aspect of the boys' existence was exempt. When the boys begged for mercy, they invariably received the reply, "Be baptized and we will leave you alone."

The boys, exhausted from working long days under brutal conditions, might be deprived of sleep until they agreed to be baptized. They would be kept awake and lectured about the glories of Christianity until they capitulated. Sometimes, children were so exhausted that they fell asleep standing upright.

In some instances, children were offered only pork to eat. Any boy who refused to eat was left to starve. Other boys were fed salted fish and forbidden to drink until they accepted baptism. Many died of this treatment, while others succumbed and accepted baptism.

Sometimes, in order to wear down the boys' resistance, the officers tried to make them eat non-kosher food. S. Beylin describes one such incident:

> They served the Cantonists *shchi* (cabbage soup containing lard). The boy avoided the shchi, though the only other food available was bread.
>
> "Jew, why aren't you eating the shchi?" the lance corporal yelled at him.
>
> "I can't. It smells of pork!"
>
> "Ah, so you're that kind. Get on your knees before the icon and be baptized!"
>
> And they held the boy in the same position for a full hour and a half until his knees grew numb. They then commanded him to stand, and proceeded to deal him fifteen or twenty strokes with the birch.[61]

The children were at the mercy of their caretakers. In deep winter in the city of Novograd, a certain priest would drive groups of naked boys out into an icy field and pour water over them. The water froze and encased them in a layer of ice.[62]

There were cases reported in which children were tied up in a sack and dropped on the ground or dragged up stairs. The most widespread form of torture was physical beating with leather straps, whips soaked in saltwater, and chunks of tree bark. The refrain was, "Agree to be baptized, or you will be beaten to death." Many boys, indeed, died as a result of injuries sustained in severe beatings.

Beatings and birchings of Cantonists occurred on a daily basis for any infringement of the rules: for wearing tzitzit, speaking Yiddish, or praying the forbidden Jewish prayers; for identifying themselves by their Jewish names instead of their new Christian names; for sneaking away from the table with a hidden piece of bread, for falling ill or wetting the bed.[63]

The Cantonists tried to conceal their wounds and cope stoically with physical pain out of fear of further punishment. A Cantonist who let on that he was in pain attracted the unwanted attention of a lance corporal, who might further beat the boy to the extent that he would be sent to the infirmary. At the infirmary, a medical corpsman would give the boy another beating. This was a punitive measure for disobedient behavior and for having received the injuries in the first place.

Bathing in rivers and lakes presented another opportunity for torturing the boys. An officer would grab a Cantonist by the head and repeatedly hold his head underwater until he nearly drowned. The child would struggle to free himself. The officer would shout, "Be baptized and I will leave you alone!" Many children became deaf from this treatment.[64]

The Cantonists were brought naked to steam baths and forced onto the hottest top steps.

"What a terrible torture!" related one Cantonist. "Children are bleeding, screaming, crying, and falling down the stairs grabbing onto other children. And on the bottom, the beatings...."

The officers would scream, "Give more steam. Let them suffocate. When will you be baptized?"[65]

Yet another form of torture required the child to stand with his feet on two separate bars and hold a heavy object. When the child was exhausted and begged to be allowed to stop, the answer was repeated, "Be baptized and I will leave you alone!"[66]

This method was described by a merchant, Victor Nankin of Tsarskoye Selo, a converted Jew from the Archangelsk Cantonists. A zealous soldier assigned to look after Nankin made him stand on the narrow sides of two adjacent beds standing far apart. He had to hold heavy pillows high above his head. The boy stood as long as he could in this unnatural position, with his arms and legs spread wide, until he fell to the floor in exhaustion, then was ordered to resume the position. This happened over and over. Each fall caused severe bruises.

When he had no strength left, he begged his torturer to let him go. The soldier replied: "Cross yourself, Jew, and I'll let you go!" Nankin said that this type of relentless physical pressure convinced him and many of his comrades to renounce Judaism and convert to Russian Orthodoxy, though they were deeply devoted to their Jewish heritage.[67]

Nankin and others provide accounts of those who accepted baptism as a result of the torture. For example, in August of 1857, a full year after the official cancellation of the Cantonist decree, one hundred and nineteen Cantonists were taken from Kiev to Odessa to be assigned to military duties. The soldiers were asked if they had any complaints. Forty-four of the baptized children from the Kiev battalion complained that they had been baptized by force. They were cross-examined and their testimony was documented in an official report. Following are excerpts from the report:

Yevesei Groikop was brought to the Kiev battalion at a young age. His commander urged him to accept baptism. When he refused, he was flogged, his finger was stabbed with a needle, and he was made to stand barefoot on a searing hot sheet of metal. On repeated occasions he was tortured for twenty-four continuous hours until he became dangerously ill. He alternated two days in the battalion with two days in the hospital. After a month of this treatment, he agreed to be baptized.[68]

Andrei Rothstein and his friends testified that they were beaten severely. When they complained to their commander, they were beaten again. Realizing that he was powerless to protect himself from this abuse, Rothstein agreed to be baptized.[69]

Lazer Gorlin and other children were ordered by the battalion commander to agree to baptism. When they refused, they were handed over to officers who made them kneel as they beat them for hours. When Gorlin complained to his commander, the commander responded by ordering that the beatings continue, stating "We can't have any Zhids here." Gorlin soon became ill and begged to be taken to the hospital. He was told that he must first agree to be baptized. He held out for two further weeks of abuse, then he agreed to baptism.[70]

Egay Marashinski's testimony is from the record of his court martial trial. He was charged with returning to the Jewish faith, having announced his intention to do so years after he underwent baptism. Marashinski stated that he was beaten on the head and his hair was torn out until his entire scalp was covered with blood.[71]

Dimitri Kaufman, also on trial for returning to Judaism, testified that he had been beaten on the hands, that needles had been inserted under his nails, and that he had been denied food for days. He withstood the torture for a month until he surrendered to the pressure to accept baptism.[72]

Marashinski and Kaufman were sentenced to hard labor for their transgression.

Resistance and Persuasion

It is difficult to ascertain the precise number of Cantonists who resisted baptism. No doubt, the policy of persuading conscripts via torture to accept baptism accomplished Tsar Nicholas's objective of increasing conversion rates. For example, over half of the Jewish children in the Saratover Cantonist Battalion between 1828–1842 (six hundred eighty seven out of one thousand three hundred and four) were forcibly baptized.[73]

The Tsar was not satisfied with the results and raised the profile of the efforts. In 1844 he instituted monthly reporting by each battalion on their progress in baptizing the Cantonists. He wrote in his own records, "Too few children are being baptized."[74]

The mandated harsher treatment of the Cantonists increased the rate of forced baptisms. One Cantonist reported that, by April 1845, all the Jewish children in the Saratover Battalion had been baptized.[75] Immediately, an additional one hundred and thirty Jewish children were brought from Kiev, and the Saratover officer wrote in June, two months later, that all the children had been baptized.[76]

The report of this wholesale baptism reached the Tsar in June 1845, to which he responded in writing, "Praise the Lord."[77]

In the Uralsker battalion, over one hundred of the three hundred and one children were baptized. In the Smolensker battalion, all the children were baptized.[78]

Former Cantonist Lentiy Isaakovich Tauber related the following:

> The pressures were well beyond the strength of nine- or ten-year-old boys to bear. I remember it as if it were today: I was spending my last year in the Cantonist barracks and was preparing to move to the soldiers' barracks, i.e., to the terrible twenty-five years' service. In early spring that year, just at the time of the Purim holiday, seventy Jewish boys from Zhitomir were brought to us in the Omsk Cantonist battalion. By Pesach [i.e. within exactly four weeks], one of them had died, sixty had been baptized, and only nine remained Jews....[79]

Even when Cantonists displayed superhuman strength and withstood torture without capitulation, there were still times when they would be dragged to church and baptized against their will. In one such case, church priests reported that Cantonists N. Zaltzkvar, N. Rozga, and A. Kutresky from Kiev had been "baptized;" according to the boys' testimony later, the priests performed no rites and sprinkled no holy water on them, but simply wrote in their report that they had been baptized.[80]

Compassion

There are stories on record of an occasional compassionate individual who showed kindness to the boys. The following was recounted by an anonymous Cantonist:

> Soon our Cantonist priest, Father Alexander, came to visit me. He brought me some presents. When I saw him, I became terribly upset... soon they would baptize me, and everything would be over... I pressed myself to Father Alexander's breast and sobbed bitterly. Kind Father Alexander sincerely tried to comfort me and talked about the joy that awaited me after baptism.
>
> "And would you, Father Alexander, cry very hard if your

son were to switch over to being a Jew?" I asked through my tears.

"You don't mean it, my child, bless you! Of course I would cry."

"But my mother will cry bitterly, too, you see, when she finds out that I have been baptized," and I cried even more bitterly.

I do not know what affected Father Alexander more — my naïve question, which at the same time seemed cunning beyond my age, or my tears, the tears of a sick young boy — but Father Alexander hurriedly left the hospital. No one bothered me after that, even when I moved back to the barracks.

From that time forward, Father Alexander, who generally had a reputation among us as a kind man, never came to us again. Soon afterward, Tsar Alexander II abolished the institution of Cantonist soldiers.

It was my cherished dream to see Father Alexander just once more. When my material circumstances improved a little, I searched for him in Omsk, but Father Alexander had vanished without a trace. I was not to see the kind priest, the witness to my sufferings, to my ardent wish to remain a Jew.[81]

Broken Soul

Some Cantonists simply cracked under the pressure. This sad account comes from the memoirs of the Yiddish writer, Yechezkel Kotik:

There was a boy in cheder named Yosele, a fine boy and an excellent student. He was an orphan, but his father had been a wealthy man. His mother was willing to pay high tuition so that her son would receive the finest education.

One day as we left the cheder for lunch, we noticed several men loitering nearby. Realizing that they were chappers, one of they boys threatened them with the nearest available weapon, which happened to be a set of candlesticks belonging to the teacher's wife. The chappers left.

Soon after, a chapper named Aaron Libl tried to grab Yosele on his way home from school. Yosele fought back and I threw a stone at Aaron Libl, which struck him in the shoulder. I took Yosele home with me. My mother agreed to let him hide with us until the danger passed. But that time never arrived. For some reason, the leaders of the Kahal specifically instructed the chappers to catch Yosele. They hid outside of Yosele's home waiting for their chance to grab him.

After weeks of hiding, Yosele so missed his mother that he struck out alone for his mother's home. En route, a chapper named Muschka grabbed him and imprisoned him in a room next to the *beit midrash* (Jewish study house). For two weeks, he languished in jail while his mother sat outside weeping. When three men entered his cell to remove him he bitterly resisted, but he was dragged outside and hoisted into a wagon. Both Yosele and his mother cried so loudly in bitter anguish that they were heard throughout the city.

Yosele was taken, starving, to the city of Brisk; his mother traveled there in another wagon. Yosele's mother was brought back from Brisk to Kaminetz and soon died.

A year later at Chanukah time, Yosele's unit arrived back in Kaminetz. I requested permission to see my old friend and a few soldiers brought him to my grandfather's home. Yosele's disheveled appearance when he entered the room stunned everyone. He was barefoot and his large overcoat reached down to his ankles. His face was swollen and pale. When we saw him we cried out, "Yosele, Yosele," but he showed no sign of response. I moved closer and again cried out his name, but it was clear that he was not coherent.

We asked the captain what had happened to Yosele. He said that when the Cantonists were sent out to central Russia, Yosele had become sick and refused to eat, just crying continuously. His officers took him to a military hospital but he still refused to eat. He kept crying until, eventually, he broke down and lost his sanity. His captain decided there was no reason to keep him in a Cantonist unit so he transferred Yosele to a new unit.[82]

Heroism

Father in Heaven who dwells on High
You are the Father of all orphans
Better to learn *Chumash* and *Rashi*
Than to eat the soldier's kasha.
Better to lie on bare wooden boards
Then to call the *yavan* "Uncle,"
Better to wear a *tallit* and *kittel*
Than to wear the Kaiser's hat.
I would rather lie ten cubits underground
Than to wear the Kaiser's sword.
I would rather lie ten cubits deep in the mud,
Than to wear the Kaiser's *kapote*.[83]
    —*popular poem from the Cantonist era*

This chapter contains accounts of Cantonists who remained Jews. Though some of the youths mentioned here were forced to accept baptism, inwardly they continued to identify as Jews.

Two Cantonists

Cantonist Yermanovich and his comrade from another company, Leib Sauda, were opinion leaders. The officers of their regiment believed that if they could persuade these two boys to accept the Russian Orthodox faith, all the Jews of both companies would follow.

The two were sent several times to Bishop Nil of Irkutsk for exhortation, but they resisted his arguments. After a visit one cold October day, the boys were taken up to the bell tower of the Bishop's church. Evidently, they were forgotten there. There were already severe frosts at that time of year, and the boys were left exposed to the elements from the evening until early morning, protected only by thin little overcoats and boots. The boys kept each other warm by pressing together all night, which saved them from death.

The bishop's servant was horrified when he chanced upon the shivering boys. He put them to bed with hot tea in his own room near the kitchen. Yermanovich's toes were frost-bitten from the cold but Sauda was uninjured.

They were taken later to Petukhov, the rector of the seminary. "Well, children, who will you be? What is your decision?" he asked them.

"We are Jews."

"Do you want to be baptized?"

"No! We want to remain Jews, like our fathers and grandfathers."

In a surprising display of compassion, the rector said, "Well, children, do exactly that. Remain Jews forever, and may the God of the Israelites be your help."[84]

Holdout

There were times when an entire battalion accepted baptism except for one individual. Such was the case with a certain Cantonist of about seventeen or eighteen years of age. Every morning, he was placed on a bench and given at least one hundred strokes with the birch. A fellow Cantonist, Israel Itzkovich, reported that he once witnessed a stream of blood flowing from this boy's head onto the ground after a beating. The boy absorbed the abuse without crying out, but he moaned in pain.

After each birching, they would send him to the infirmary, treat his wounds and then beat him again.

This particular Cantonist was saved by the ascent of Tsar Alexander II to the throne. Soon afterward, on August 26, 1856, an imperial command was issued which dissolved the battalions and half-battalions of Cantonist soldiers. The eighteen-year-old Cantonist, who had never renounced his faith, was transferred from the ranks of the Cantonists to the Archangelsk garrison battalion.[85]

Sergei Mosayov

Cantonist Sergei Mosayov was a frail child who was baptized against his will in 1850. His official age in the baptism records was fifteen; several years were often added to the boys' real ages when they were baptized.

Sergei was determined not to betray his faith and he continued to observe as many Jewish rites and rituals as he could. The priest's exhortations fell on deaf ears. Sergei remained steadfast. He was sent to a monastery so that his bad influence would not 'contaminate' the other children.

In November 1850, the commissar ordered him transferred to another church where he would be supervised by monks. Mosayov became sick during the journey and was hospitalized in Moscow. He arrived at the church in 1851.

The treatment toward "sinners" in church was worse than in jail, yet the physically weak child had the spiritual strength to survive the most terrifying tortures, year after year. The bi-annual reports on his status never varied: Mosayov was determined to remain a Jew and he refused to make any declarations that could be interpreted as acceptance of his initial forced baptism.

This continued for over seven years. The more they tortured him, the stronger he became. Finally, his commanders accepted that he was a hopeless case and gave up trying to convert him. He was sent to a regiment in Siberia. The long battle they had waged against the child soldier was futile. Sergei Mosayov triumphed in the end.[86]

Yaakov Moisyevich Iertsel

Cantonist Yaakov Moisyevich Iertsel of Irkutsk was forcibly baptized. Like many others, he remained loyal to his Jewish heritage and maintained his Jewish convictions. His story is not unlike that of many Marranos, who during Catholic Inquisitional rule, accepted Christianity but secretly remained observant Jews.

Here is Iertsel's account, told years later.

> I do not even know myself how I remained a Jew. When I remember the past, I relive that whole nightmare. First they whipped me because I ran away to town without permission, to see my fellow Jews. Then they whipped me for some childish misbehavior of fighting with a comrade. When I was threatened with a third whipping, I could not hold out and I finally agreed to be baptized. That got me out

of the whipping.

There was a custom of christening everyone who consented to baptism with a new Christian name. I was christened Alexander. However, in my heart I stayed a Jew and thus, I still felt myself to be Yaakov.

I do not even know what powerful force held me in its grip but I continued to feel myself a Jew. A nationalist instinct, the tears of my mother who begged me, an eight-year-old boy, to remain a Jew, or a natural resistance to those whom I could not avoid considering my enemies.... After I agreed to be baptized, I fell ill from grief, and they put me in the hospital."[87]

Pesach Shkolba

One October day in 1845, a cruel officer named Yefremov was beating a Cantonist. He threatened Shkolba, "You will be next!"

Shkolba begged the officer to show mercy to the other child. Yefremov, in response, turned on Shkolba and struck him in the face with an iron bar. In a fit of rage, Shkolba threw himself on Yefremov and tore the badge off his shoulder, then fled with it.

Shkolba took the badge to the commander and reported how Yefremov constantly tortured him. The commander was not moved. Neither was the military tribunal that ordered the boy to run the gauntlet, be beaten one thousand strokes, and suffer life imprisonment.[88]

Escape

"Only two of us, Afanasiy Stepanov and I, are still alive from our Archangelsk Battalion. Three knifed themselves, two hanged themselves, and several drowned themselves."

The author of this 1845 account recorded that when he could no longer tolerate the torture, he had submitted to baptism.[89]

Berke Finklestein

When Cantonist Berke Finkelstein was brought to his battalion, he refused to eat army food or to listen to lectures on Russian Orthodoxy.

Once, he swore in the presence of his commander that he would never give up his allegiance to Judaism. The commander laughed at him.

"You think we are afraid of your oath? No problem. Once we beat you two hundred strokes with a whip, you will become a devoted Christian."

Finkelstein looked into the commander's eyes and replied, "You can starve me or kill me, but I will never give up my religion."

None of the other Cantonists believed that Berke would be able to withstand the torture. But no matter how severely he was tortured, he remained steadfast. The officers would throw him, barefoot, on burning coals, hang him upside-down, and make him run naked on the ice in the bitter cold. Yet Berke remained loyal to his heritage.

Once, two heavy sacks of sand were tied to Finkelstein's neck and a gun held to his head. He was ordered to stand motionless for three hours and warned that if he sat or kneeled, he would be beaten a hundred times until he could stand no more.

Berke stood until he had turned white and pale, then collapsed to the ground and was beaten. The soldiers guarding him wanted to beat him further, but Finkelstein had already fainted and was in a coma.

An hour later, the commander called for a doctor, who managed with great effort to revive Finkelstein. The commander ordered the guards to remove the sacks of sand and leave the "fanatic" alone. The commander acknowledged, "He would rather give up his life than his religion."

Finkelstein remained a proud Jew. After a few months his wounds healed, and by the end of the year he was regarded as an exemplary Cantonist.

Another Cantonist wrote, "Many years later, I found Berke Finkelstein in another city, far away. He was married with a large family and presided over a grocery store. I asked him, 'Remember how you stood barefoot on hot coals and sacks of sand were tied to your neck?' Berke replied, 'Oh, how I remember. These things may not be forgotten. We must tell them to our children and grandchildren.'"[90]

Before the Tsar's Eyes
The following story is probably legend, meant to illustrate that the goal of the Tsar, to achieve the mass conversion of the Cantonists and, eventually, of all the Jews of the Pale of Settlement, would never be realized.

It has been told that when the army commanders in Kazan were preparing a military review for Tsar Nicholas I, they wanted to impress him. They redoubled their efforts to convert the Jewish Cantonists of the local battalions. However, all the efforts of the commanders were in vain.

They resorted to a risky public display. On the occasion of a visit by Tsar Nicholas I, several hundred Jewish Cantonists were taken to the river, where the clergy were waiting in full vestments. Everything had been prepared for the performance of the rite of baptism in his presence. The soldiers stood motionless.

The Tsar drove up. After the usual formalities, he ordered the children to wade into the water to accept baptism.

"Yes sir, Your Imperial Majesty!" the Jewish children cried with one voice.

Nicholas was amazed at this enthusiasm. But after the water had covered the children, there were only ripples and bubbles. The children did not re-emerge. They had drowned themselves, choosing death over baptism.

Nicholas, the legend adds, grabbed his head in horror and tore his hair. The heart spoke, even in this formidable tsar! The Cantonists, exhausted by prolonged tortures, had apparently made a secret pact to end their lives in the presence of the Tsar, to the glory of God — *al kiddush Hashem* (in sanctification of God's name).[91]

Resistance, Revolt, and Rescue

The Cantonist era saw schisms within many Jewish communities. The Kahal's leadership was sometimes challenged by other leaders and members of the community. Jews were pitted against each other.

This chapter describes incidents involving members of the community taking a moral stand against cooperation with the authorities in an attempt to save Jews from a life as Cantonist soldiers.

Revolt in Mirrer

Rabbi Baruch HaLevi Epstein recorded his grandfather's role in leading the community's revolt against the Kahal in the city of Mirrer, Poland.

Adapted from Baruch HaLevi Epstein's book Mekor Baruch, published in Vilna in 1874.[92]

The evil reached its heights in the city where my elderly grandfather lived. Those souls not poisoned by this cruelty could not bear to see more of it. They could not stand the moans of infants who had been sacrificed on the altar of the sinners.

A group of dignitaries consulted with the honored rabbi of their city and decided that, once and for all, they had to put an end to this sin. Finally, rabbinic permission was granted, and they called the members of the Jewish community for liberation of the captives. The dignitaries appealed to each individual to judge for himself and to rise up as one entity against the tyranny of evildoers.

With a strong hand, the masses forced open the doors of the community room that had been used by the Kahal leaders to imprison little chicks, small children, tender infants who had not even left the bosom of their mothers and the knees of their fathers. They found the children lying like bound calves with only shirts upon their flesh, their long tzitz-it reaching down to their small feet.

The voice of death mingled with their chirping and their soft, inno-cent sighs. The children did not know nor comprehend what it all was about. They were puzzled, as if asking themselves, "We are innocent lambs, what sins have we committed?" Seeing them in that hell was ter-rible and painful and of boundless sorrow.

Suddenly, abruptly, beyond their wildest dreams, the chains of the prisoners were broken and they were called to freedom and to rejoin their families. My grandfather stood at the head of the group of digni-taries. He was an influential man and highly respected among the resi-dents of the city, so he spoke on their behalf.

The city administrators and officials considered my grandfather a great and honorable man. For this reason, they did not bring charges against him. In their heart of hearts, the townspeople harbored kind feel-ings and mercy. The daily and open actions of wicked people distressed them as well. They viewed this extreme action as an appropriate response to the crisis, a gesture toward restoration of justice and honor.

But the bloodthirsty tyrants were not calmed just because their prey was pulled from their mouths. They complained to the court in Minsk about my grandfather for having taken the law into his own hands. The court summoned him to appear and give an account of the situation and his actions.

The day he left to stand trial, the whole town worried and mourned. Everyone cried, old and young, women and men. The rabbi and city elders called for a day of fasting and prayer to God on my grandfather's behalf so that he would suffer no evil. According to the elders who remember the events and tell the story, that day became a Day of Judgment for all. On that day, the storekeeper left his business and the artisan left his work. Everyone was united in concern for my grandfa-ther's welfare. They prayed for him to return home quickly and in peace. When the sinning evildoers saw the great emotion that gripped the peo-ple of the city, many of them left town, fearing for their own welfare.

When my grandfather described to the judges how these people lacked any human compassion and how much suffering and distress they had caused, he was acquitted, freed, and allowed to go in peace.

Revolt at Oshitz

Jewish informers spied and eavesdropped to collect information valuable to the government or to the Kahal and their chappers. The informers presented a real and present danger to the community.

Over the centuries, many prominent rabbinical authorities have sanctioned the execution of informers. Assassinations of informers by other Jews occurred during this era as well.

One such case transpired in the city of Oshitz. This incident and its trauma demonstrate the extent of the grip of Tsar Nicholas upon Russian Jewry.

Adapted from Saul M. Ginsburg's 1915 Historical Work: Jewish Martyrdom in Tsarist Russia[93]

One of the greatest threats that faced Jewish communities came from informers from within. Informers were especially dangerous during the era of Nicholas I, when Jewish communities attempted to conceal eligible recruits from the government. During this period, the official Russian government position was that every Jew was responsible to inform on his fellow Jew. And there was no lack of informers.

The community itself often took action against the informer. The town rabbi would summon the congregation to synagogue, candles would be lit, and the informer would be excommunicated. After his death, he would not be buried in a Jewish cemetery and no tombstone would be erected. Thus, he would be forever cut off from his Jewish brothers.

The following story of the events in the city of Oshitz is well known as a gruesome tale of torture of the martyrs who paid with their lives for the community's action against informers.

In 1836 in the Oshitzer province, there lived two Jewish tile manufacturers named Shwartzman and Oxman. To curry favor with the authorities in their city, they often informed on their fellow Jews. Yet, as long as they caused no serious harm, the Jews left them alone.

The debilitating poverty and heavy burden of government taxes, along with the threat of conscription, prompted many Jews to go into hiding. Not only would they escape conscription, but the Jewish community would have to pay their share of the taxes. Since these people did not legally exist, they could not work. Oshitz had many such "hidden ones" who lived in concealment from the day they first evaded the draft until the ends of their lives.

The government knew of the existence of these Jews but without inside information, was powerless to ascertain their whereabouts. When they obtained proof of the existence of the hidden Jews, the entire community was in mortal danger and the authorities would raise taxes tenfold.

Shwartzman's and Oxman's unscrupulousness in informing on fellow Jews threatened to place the Oshitz community in grave danger. The leaders of the Jewish community bribed them to remain silent. In return, they blackmailed the community leaders with exorbitant demands. To prove that they meant business, the two informed on several individuals. The situation became critical.

In February 1836, it was clear that something had to be done to prevent these two informers from bringing tragedy upon the Jews of the entire area. The rabbinic leadership of the Jewish community gathered to discuss the threat. Rav Michoel Averbach of Duyanevetz took part in these discussions. Some claim that the Rav Yisroel Friedman of Rizhin gave his consent.

The rabbis decided to hire hit men to dispose of the informers. Every member of the community contributed to pay the assassins who would murder Shwartzman and Oxman.

The hit men were hired and the deed was done. Shwartzman was choked and his body was burned in the Oshitzer bathhouse. Oxman was killed in the forest near Duyanevetz and his body was lowered into the river with stones tied to his neck.

An investigation ensued, headed by Detective Graf Gureyev. The cohesiveness among the Jews was such that everyone in Oshitz knew the truth but all remained silent. Doctors were bribed to turn a deaf ear. Even the wives and children of the murdered informers feigned ignorance of their whereabouts.

The investigation continued. Tsar Nicholas constantly demanded updates about the case. Detective Gureyev, understanding that this was his big chance to earn the Tsar's favor, threw himself into the investigation and sent monthly progress reports.

By July of 1836, fifty Jews of the Oshitzer district had been arrested and imprisoned in Duyanevetz. They were held in solitary confinement in a heavily guarded convent surrounded by stone walls.

After months of both psychological and physical torture, the prisoners finally began to talk. Eventually, the story was pieced together and clarified. More and more people were implicated and arrested.

In August, the Duyanevetzer Rav was arrested and his books were sent to Vilna for the censor's review. The censor identified and translated the section of the *Shulchan Aruch* (Code of Jewish Law) dealing with the subject of informers within the Jewish community, which states that execution of an informer is permitted. The authorities thus concluded that the informers had been killed with the consent of the rabbinic leadership.

Detective Gureyev hesitated to arrest the Rizhiner Rebbe because he knew that his arrest would arouse the anger of the Jews throughout the district. In a report to Nicholas, Gureyev wrote, "Because of the great political power of *Hasidus* (the Hasidic movement), the Rabbis have powerful authority over the community and the Jewish internal organizations." However, by September, Gureyev had decided to arrest the Rebbe.

The solved case in Oshitz was a breakthrough for Nicholas. It served as a justification to torture Jews throughout Russia in order to break the web of silence that had previously protected them. This development sent fear into the hearts of Jews all over Russia.

In March of 1837, Tsar Nicholas appointed a special military commission to judge the prisoners and all others who had been involved. Nicholas wanted the investigation to be held in Kaminetz but it possessed no jail large enough to hold all the defendants, so the trial took place in Duyanevetz.

On July 27, 1837, the military tribunal opened its proceedings. Eighty Jews, four Christians, and many peasants were called to testify. The witnesses included influential leaders of several Jewish Community Councils as well as *parnasim* (leaders) of the district. The Duyanevetzer and Rizhiner Rebbes were adjudicated. Many of those called to testify were respected elders; countless others escaped before they could be called.

The trial lasted for eighteen months. At its conclusion, the military commission handed over the case to the Ministry of Defense, and the case languished for another year.

In 1840, four years after the suspects had been arrested, Nicholas signed the sentence. All had expected severe punishment, but the sentence exceeded their wildest nightmares. The military had decided to punish the Jews in the same manner in which the Jewish community had punished the informers. Even in those days, such punitive measures evoked outrage throughout Russia.

Six of the Jews, two of whom were aged seventy, were sentenced to one to two thousand lashes, running the gauntlet, and five hundred beatings. Of the nine people who knew about the killings and were involved, seven received one thousand lashes. Many others were sentenced to life imprisonment and two elderly Jews were sent to Siberia. Eight people who knew the story but did not inform the government were given five hundred lashes each, and one received three hundred lashes. The Duyanevetzer Rav was sent to Siberia.

Many of the arrested Jews from Oshitz had been desperate to save the Rizhiner Rebbe, taking the full blame on themselves so that the Rebbe would not be implicated. The Rizhiner Rebbe, who had already spent several years in jail, was declared innocent and released.

Most of those who were lashed and beaten died on the spot.

Rabbi Shik Battles the Chappers
The noted Rabbi Ilya Ben Binyamin Shik waged an ongoing battle against the chappers and their accomplices. His exploits were legendary.
> *The first of these accounts involving Rabbi Shik was adapted from D. Pines in* Battles Against the Chappers, *published in 1915 in* Yevreiskaya Starina.[94] *The second incident was adapted from A.S. Friedberg's 1903 article* Remembrances of my Youth, *and the* Book of Kobrin, *edited by B. Schwartz and I.C. Biletsky, published in Israel in 1951.[95]*

The righteous Rabbi Eliyahu Shik was aware that the Kahal leaders from the town of Volkovysk were particularly cruel. They turned in substitute recruits, not only in place of another person who was due for induction, but also years before that person would be scheduled for summons to serve.

Once, in Grodno, Rabbi Shik encountered a wealthy man and principal leader of the Kahal from the town of Volkovysk. The rabbi categorically demanded that the abuse of authority and the hunting down of defenseless children be halted immediately. The rich and influential man refused, and in response the rabbi slapped his face twice.

The enraged town boss made use of his connections to bring the matter to the attention of the governor and, as a result, the rabbi was jailed. However, the popularity of the rabbi and the angry rumbling of the general public forced the leader of the Volkovysk community to petition for the release of the man who had insulted him.

At that time, the heads of the Kahal in the town of Mirrer had issued a new decree to ambush any traveler passing through the town and search him for travel papers. If someone had neglected to equip himself with his papers when setting out on his journey, or even if his identity papers were one day past their expiration date, the traveler would be seized as a piyamnike to fill the community's army conscription quota. The unscrupulous individuals who turned him in might exchange him as ransom for their own sons or relatives, or receive a cash reward from the community fund for contributing a conscript to the quota. Because of these inducements, the ranks of the chappers increased.

Many Jews at the time lived by trading, which required traveling from place to place, and no one could be certain that he would not be snatched.

Two weeks after he was released from jail, Rabbi Shik came to the town of Mirrer. The rabbi, in his righteousness, realized the terrible damage that was being done and he made a great noise against the evil people.

He went to the courtyard of the synagogue. "My fellow Jews!" he cried. "Why are you silent? Come and let us save Jewish souls!"

There was a great tumult when he proposed that the community revolt against the Kahal leaders, wreak havoc upon their community house and raze it to the ground. Everyone grabbed a hatchet or an ax and followed the rabbi to the Kahal building housing the captives. The mob forced their way into the building, broke down the doors, cut the bonds of the captives and freed them.

The rabbi called the dignitaries of the Kahal to the synagogue. He made them swear on a Torah scroll from the Holy Ark that they would never repeat such abominations against their fellow Jews.

Righteous Congregation
Rav Yankele Boisker drew a parallel to a Biblical commandment in an attempt to encourage this congregation to take action against its community leaders.

Adapted from Abraham Lewin, Cantonists: About Jewish Recruits in Russia During the Era of Tsar Nicholas I, 1827–1855, published in Warsaw in 1934.[96]

Once, the famous rabbi Rav Yankele Boisker joined the congregation of Neizager for the Sabbath. In the middle of the silent recitation prayer, a desperate widow stormed into the men's section of the synagogue, weeping furiously. Her only child had just been taken from her home to take the place of the child of a wealthy man who had paid bribe money to the Kahal.

The head of the community, unmoved by her tears, yelled to his assistant to throw her out of the synagogue. The assistant complied and the poor woman was ejected.

Just then, the elderly, distinguished Rav Boisker strode up to the ark and removed a Torah scroll.

"Holy Torah," he proclaimed in a loud voice, "from you we learn the commandment of *Shiluach HaKan,* of sending away the mother bird before taking her offspring [*Deuteronomy* 22:7]. Dear Torah, I am nearly eighty years old. Until today, when my own eyes witnessed this tragedy, I have never seen such a thing actually occur. Your people have cruelly thrown away the mother and taken the child. May the congregation be repaid for their deeds both in this world and in the next."

His words inflamed the congregation with righteous anger. Together, they surged out of the synagogue and stormed the community building, broke open the door and freed the captive child.

The Tzemach Tzedek

The Lubavitcher Hasidim, also known as Chabad, distinguished themselves in their work on behalf of the Cantonists. Chabad publications recount some of these incidents. These sources are taken from 'Kehot Publishers' and are recounted here with their permission.

> These accounts are adapted from books published by Chabad. Rabbi Menachem Mendel Schneerson, the Tzemach Tzedek, wrote Derech Mitzvosecha. Rabbi Abraham Glitzenstein wrote Our Master and Teacher, The Tzemach Tzedek; Igros Kodesh. The Tzemach Tzedek is the volume on Rabbi Schneerson in the Igros Kodesh compilation.

In 1827, Rabbi Menachem Mendel Schneerson (1789–1866), who went by the pen name Tzemach Tzedek, succeeded his father-in-law as Lubavitcher Rebbe.

The Tzemach Tzedek organized committees to pursue all feasible avenues to aid the Cantonists. One committee assisted communities to obtain reductions in their conscript quotas. A second, *Chevra Techias*

HaMaisim (Society of the Resurrection of the Dead), ransomed conscripted children by bribing Russian officials to officially list children as deceased; the children were quickly sent far away to safe refuge. The third committee sent its representatives to the assembly points for Jewish Cantonists to comfort the children and encourage them to remain loyal Jews; they also disbursed funds to the children, sometimes the only money in the children's possession when they departed for years in the service.

Those who engaged in these activities did so at great personal risk. If caught, they faced charges of sedition and severe penalties.[97]

In another incident, a Jewish informer relayed information to the Governor of Vitebsk that the Tzemach Tzedek had sent an emissary, Rabbi Aharon of Bilinich, to communities in the districts of Mohliv and Vitebsk. The emissary was instructing Kahal leaders (many of whom, in that area, were righteous and protected Jewish boys at great risk) to oust the chappers from their cities.

The Governor informed the Minister of the Interior of a meeting to be convened in Petersburg for the purpose of entrapping the Tzemach Tzedek so that he could be prosecuted for sedition. However, as a cover story, they also invited Rabbi Yitzchak of Volozhin, Rabbi Yehudah Halpern, and the *Maskil* (member of the Emancipation movement) Yehudah Shtern. The plan was to entrap the Rebbe, who would attend the meeting where his movements would be limited and he could be closely watched by the authorities.[98]

Rabbi Zev Wolf, fearing the potential danger to the Rebbe, attempted to dissuade him from attending the scheduled meeting. His efforts did not deter the Tzemach Tzedek from attending, nor did the threats to the Rebbe's personal safety deter him from continuing to send emissaries to aid the Cantonists, and to call for the ousting of chappers from cities.[99]

Betrayal and Rescue

This is the story of Reb Chaim Yehoshua, a disciple of the Tzemach Tzedek, who worked to obtain the release of Cantonists.

Adapted from: Rabbi Avraham Persan, Sefer HaTamim, *published in Brooklyn in 1972.*

The Hasid Reb Chaim Yehoshua was in the area of Kazan for four months. He conducted business in the town and was thus quite familiar with the ways of the village folk. He often traveled on business from one small village to another to ransom children.

Some children fled on their own after they were freed. Others needed help to escape, and Reb Chaim found them places of refuge.

Reb Chaim Yehoshua was clever in carrying out his mission. When he first arrived in a village, he would purchase some products in the market, such as wool and linen, to mask the purpose of his visit in the guise of a business trip. Then, as if out of casual interest, he would make inquiries about the young boys of the vicinity.

One day, a Jew who spoke Yiddish with a Vohlynian accent came to the village of Kazan where Reb Chaim was staying. He also feigned the appearance of a wool-and-linen merchant having come to purchase the local goods, and he and Reb Chaim soon became friends and lodged together for about a month. In truth, the man was there to spy on Reb Chaim, whom he soon discovered was engaged in the rescue of Cantonist recruits.

At the time, Reb Chaim Yehoshua had rescued eight boys and had not yet found safe places for them. Some of the boys were with him in Kazan. The others were in nearby towns, begging for food. His "friend" assisted him in ransoming the Cantonists and in making additional arrangements for them. Reb Chaim thus managed to find places for six of the children in Kazan, and he decided to take the other two home with him when he left.

On the day that Reb Chaim Yehoshua was scheduled to leave, three armed soldiers appeared along with the merchant from Vohlynia. They arrested Reb Chaim and bound him in chains. When the two children saw the soldiers, they fled for their lives and alerted the other children who were in hiding in the city. All disappeared.

For seven months, Reb Chaim Yehoshua was moved in chains from one military jail to another while he awaited trial for sedition. Finally, he was brought to Vitebsk.[100]

The Tzemach Tzedek was determined to assist in gaining Reb Yehoshua's freedom. He sent a letter to another activist, Rabbi Zev Wolf, with instructions to treat this as a special case and direct all efforts toward Yehoshua's release. Wolf, who ordinarily performed rescue activities in a rational and unemotional manner, was instructed by the

Tzemach Tzedek in his letter to operate in this case with particular passion since Reb Yehoshua had rescued hundreds of boys.

Pressure on key officials yielded success. Reb Yehoshua was allowed contact with friends who brought him kosher provisions during his incarceration. Ultimately, Reb Yehoshua's case was transferred to a civilian court where his sentence was far lighter than the potential sentence of the military court.[101]

Escape

There are some accounts of escape attempts by Cantonists. Such attempts were seldom successful, but an occasional story of escape ends in triumph.

Escape or the assistance of escapees brought serious consequences. To facilitate capture, the police were provided with a complete description of an escaped Cantonist, including birthmarks and open wounds. Once recaptured, an example was made of the escapees. They were often beaten to death.

Any Jew found hiding a recruit or helping one escape would himself be held as a recruit. Those unfit for army service would be sentenced to hard labor or exiled to Siberia. There was also collective punishment. A Jewish community that harbored a fugitive faced a stiff monetary fine.[102]

Aborted Flight

At the bustling corner of Nemetskaya and Trokskaya Streets in the city of Vilna, a strapping young Jew was wrangling excitedly with a little soldier. He was a new conscript who had just run away from his barracks. The soldier was the barracks guard who had spotted the escape attempt and pursued the fugitive. He begged the young recruit to return to the barracks. The Jew, pale as death, ground his teeth, looked at the soldier with revulsion and turned to make a run for it, but was blocked by the arrival of a second soldier. Even two guards could not restrain the boy.

A crowd of curious onlookers gathered. Convinced that he would not be able to slip away, the fugitive took firm hold of the door of a nearby store; the soldiers tried in vain to tear him from it.

Suddenly, two burly chappers appeared as if they had sprung from nowhere. When he saw them, the fugitive began to shake like a leaf. The chappers were reluctant to resort to force in front of the whole crowd. One of them stood behind the soldiers, as though to back them up, while the other ran to the barracks for reinforcements. Together, all the guards managed to tear the fugitive away from the door and send him back to the barracks. Since the unfortunate fellow continued to resist, the soldiers pushed him forward while pummeling him with healthy punches.[103]

Cover-up

A Cantonist named Kretchmar related that he escaped, only to be found shortly after. He was brutally beaten and taken to a hospital, where he stayed for four months. Somehow, he miraculously survived his injuries. Throughout his hospitalization, the doctors recorded in his medical record on the board near his bed that his suffering was due to tuberculosis.[104]

Brutality

On one occasion, in March 1848, a Cantonist escaped and was caught two days later. The commander of his battalion took him to his home for interrogation. He beat the boy on the head with an iron pipe and broke his skull. The escapee was also beaten with sticks and whips and with a gun handle, until the gun broke. A few hours later, he died of his beatings.[105]

Successful Escape

One rainy day, a motley group of thirty Cantonists was passing through the town of Koritz when they stopped to rest. They were on their way north to a farming village to be raised by local peasants.

The frightened children were exhausted and soaked to the bone, hungry and weak from grueling travel. Their guards, older soldiers, entered the first Jewish home they saw and demanded that they be allowed to rest there for the night. The soldiers ignored the family's protests that there were larger homes in the village and evicted them for the night. The young Cantonists collapsed on the floor in their clothes and fell into an exhausted slumber. The old soldiers drank some vodka, emptied the food pantry, and fell asleep as well.

At daybreak, the soldiers awakened the children. They counted heads and discovered that one child was missing. The others insisted that they knew nothing of his whereabouts. The wet clothes of the missing child lay in a heap on the ground, but he was nowhere to be seen. The soldiers searched the home and warned its inhabitants that they would face severe measures if they did not deliver the child, but to no avail. All day they searched the village, but the child seemed to have vanished into thin air.

Toward nightfall, the soldiers gave up and departed with the children. The homeowner and his family moved back into their house.

"Maybe he is in the chimney," suggested one of the children. They opened the trap door to the chimney. There he huddled, hungry and frightened, but alive!

"Who are you?" they asked him.

The boy said that he was an only child. He had been torn away from his parents' arms, and his mother had run after him and tried desperately to save him. Now he had managed to save himself.

The master of the house sent the child back home to his mother, laden with baskets of food.[106]

The Aftermath

There were men in Polotzk whose faces made you old in a minute. They had served Nicholas I, and came back unbaptized.
From The Promised Land *by Mary Antin*[107]

On February 19, 1855, Tsar Nicholas died. The news and celebrations spread rapidly throughout the Pale of Settlement.

Upon the coronation of Alexander II in February 1856, the Jewish community sent a report to the new Tsar detailing the abuse that children had suffered as a result of the Cantonist Decree and requesting of him to take action to improve their situation.

Alexander dealt promptly with the matter. He issued orders that incrementally abolished the Cantonist Decree. On August 25, he ordered the ending of conscription of underage recruits and reduced the quota of Jewish recruits to an equal proportion to the rest of the population.[108] On December 25 of that year, Alexander issued another decree which, "restored to the families of soldiers the right to make arrangements for their sons at their own discretion."[109]

The worst aspects of the scourge of the Cantonist system were over. The Kahal was required to supply recruits, mainly adults, until 1874, when the decree was fully abolished and the length of a military term was limited to five years.

In Praise of the Cantonists
The Tzemach Tzedek compared the suffering of the Cantonists to the persecution of the Jews during the days of Hellenist Greek[110] rule because it was of a spiritual nature.

"We cannot imagine the greatness of praying and chanting psalms by the Cantonists. It is worth more in heaven than the intention and fervor of the Arizal.[111] Their prayers are full of self-sacrifice and simple faith."

"A learned man comes to the realization that he must keep the Torah," explained the Rebbe. "However, the Cantonists knew this from pure and simple faith. When the Messiah comes, he will be inspired by these young Jews who sacrificed so much. There will be a separate place for these Jews. Even the most honest and sincere Jews will be jealous of them."

Reb Chaim, a follower of the Tzemach Tzedek and a Talmudic scholar in his own right, once asked him, "Rebbe, how does one become a simple self-sacrificing Jew?"

The Rebbe replied, "It is more difficult to be a self-sacrificing Jew than to know the entire Talmud."[112]

Yom Kippur

Once a group of illiterate Cantonists who had become regular soldiers were quartered in a Jewish city on Yom Kippur. They came to the synagogue to pray.

When the time for the *Neilah* (concluding) service arrived, one of the Cantonists was sent to the front of the Synagogue to lead the prayers. Since he had been drafted in early childhood and had nearly completed his twenty-five years of service, he was unmarried and had no family.

The Cantonist stood before the congregation and cried out, "Father in Heaven, for what shall I pray? I cannot pray for children because I never married and now have no hope of raising a family. I am too old to start anew. I cannot pray for life, for of what value is such a life? It would be preferable to die. I cannot pray for a livelihood because Nicholas provides for my daily bread. The only thing I can pray for is *Yisgadal V'yiskadash Shmei Rabboh* (May His great Name grow exalted and sanctified; the first line of the mourner's prayer)."

The congregation heard this heartfelt prayer and burst into tears.[113]

Encounter with the Chafetz Chaim

The great luminary the Chafetz Chaim (Rabbi Yisrael Meir HaCohen of Radin) often traveled among cities.

Once at an inn in Vilna, he saw a burly Jew sitting at a table and ordering the serving girl to bring him a portion of roast goose and a glass of whisky. Without first making the blessing, he devoured the meal. He spoke coarsely to the serving girl. The Chafetz Chaim observed him from a corner and was about to approach the man and rebuke him for his behavior. The innkeeper rushed over to prevent the Chafetz Chaim from approaching the fellow. He feared that the man, a simple and uneducated individual, a former soldier for Tsar Nicholas, might be rude to the sainted rabbi or even strike him.

"Please, Rabbi, leave him alone. You cannot talk to this type of person. He is very crude. He is a true boor who knows no other way. When he was seven years old, he was abducted with other child Cantonists and dragged off to Siberia. Until the age of eighteen, he lived among farmers, and then he served in the army of Nicholas for twenty-five years. In schools like those, could he have learned anything better? Is it any wonder that he is crude, wild, and base? He was out of a Jewish environment for over thirty years. He didn't learn one letter of Torah. Judaism was alien to him. It would be best if you did not start with him. I value your honor too much."

A calm, affectionate smile radiated from the face of the Chafetz Chaim. "Such a Jew! Don't worry. I know how to speak to him. I just hope good will come of the conversation."

The Chafetz Chaim approached the man and greeted him, "*Shalom aleichem* (Peace be with you). Is what I heard about you true — that as a boy you were kidnapped and dragged off to Siberia? That you grew up among the gentiles and did not learn even one letter of the Torah? You went through hell in this world. You endured nightmares, persecution, and torture. The evil ones tried more than once to get you to leave your faith. They forced you to eat pig and non-kosher food. Nonetheless you remained a Jew. You did not convert."

"How fortunate I would be," he continued, "if I had merits like yours that entitled me to the rewards of the next world as yours do. Your place in the world-to-come will be among the greatest and most pious Torah scholars. Your sacrifice and devotion is no trivial matter. You suffered for over thirty years for the sake of Judaism and heaven. This was a greater trial then that of Chanania, Mishael, and Azaria."[114]

Tears welled up in the former soldier's eyes. He was moved by the warm and good-hearted outpourings from this pure living wellspring whose words had refreshed his weary spirit. When he realized who was speaking to him, he broke into tears and kissed the hands of the Chafetz Chaim.

The Chafetz Chaim continued, "A man like you deserves to be amidst those holy Jews who gave their lives to sanctify God's name. If you would be an observant Jew for the remainder of your life, no one would be more fortunate than you."

This man remained with the Chafetz Chaim until he became a fully observant Jew.[115]

Yehudah Leib Levin:
Loss of Innocence

This recollection by Yehudah Leib Levin recalls the chappers and the tumult they caused within Jewish communities.[116]

The year 1854 was a year of trouble and rebuke for Israel. It was the year of the "captives." I was a youth of nine then, living in my parents' home in Minsk, the city in which I was born.

One summer day, when I arrived at my religious teacher's room, the teacher was not there and the room was empty. The landlady told me that he was hiding from the chappers. The other children were also confined to their homes because the danger had increased for everyone, both young and old. Babies were snatched from their cradles, bridegrooms from under the *chupa* [wedding canopy] and the elderly from their homes, for delivery to the army.

I returned to my father's house and nobody was there but the servant, who was cooking. My mother and sister stayed in the shop that whole day, and my father was preoccupied with business affairs. I wanted to go into one of the rooms in the house but its doors were closed.

"What is happening today?" I asked myself. I stood bewildered until my eyes adjusted to the darkness. I saw a grown man with a beard sprawled prostrate on the floor. I looked more closely and recognized Reb Feyvish, the baker. I was struck by the fear of God, and I shouted out, "Oya!"

The servant hurried in, grabbed my arm, pulled me from the room and locked its doors. She was angry and nervous. I stood frenzied and fearful, my heart pounding. I pleaded with the servant to tell me what was going on. She made me swear to keep the secret, then told me that Reb Feyvish was hiding in our home from the chappers. I had already seen chappers and I knew that young children were being taken to the army, but would they take Reb Feyvish too? He was a dignitary with a full beard!

I was seeing a bearded man, a father, hiding like a child in a dark room, flat on the floor, and here I am free, going wherever I please. Reb Feyvish, the baker, with whose son I had often played, was now lowered in my eyes. But my compassion was soon aroused by seeing this father with a beard floundering on the ground in a dark room. I felt sword pricks in my heart and a dull pain. If it were, heaven forbid, my father lying on the ground in the room of a stranger — then my mother and sisters would cry bitterly, and I would be howling and moaning as well. And that must have been how Reb Feyvish's children were crying, and how his wife was wailing. I was sorry both for them and for him, the poor father.

I asked the servant if I could bring Reb Feyvish his meals from his house every day, and she agreed. So every day I would go down the road to the riverbank to his house. The street was totally deserted. Almost all the owners of the houses were hiding wherever they could.

Coming from one building was a tumult and din. It was the inn where abducted Jews were being held. There the old army people were gathered, the diadke with their young protégés, the children of Israel, infants who had already been handed over to the army. Their heads were shaven and they wore round Russian hats that were much too large for them. They wore Russian coats that hung to the ground and got twisted up in their legs as they walked.

Like all the children of my age, I was terrified of any army personnel. "Russia" was for me a symbol of shock and horror into whose image I was cast. "Russia" had a way of beating everything it came upon with an evil fist, and it undoubtedly beat these tender children, who were beautiful and forlorn. How beautiful could they be with a head without peyot? How miserable they looked because their heads did not have peyot! My heart went out to them. I felt a little frightened of the "Russian" children, but it so happened that when our glances crossed, I saw tears gleaming in their eyes and I began to cry as well. But a diadke glared at me with eyes emanating black fire and I fled in haste.

I was relatively calm and personally did not fear the chappers, because my father was an important landlord, distinguished in Torah and highly regarded by everyone. My mother was the daughter of the most famous *tzaddik* (righteous person) of his generation, Rabbi Moshe Kabrina'ar. And I, I was one of the "good children," a prodigy, the likes of whom were not touched by the hand of the masses. Free both of fear and of school-work, because the teachers and pupils had all gone into hiding and the *chedarim* [schools] were closed, I wandered daily around the city streets seeing the little "Russians," and my heart burst when I realized they were in the hands of non-Jews, who forced them to eat pork — oh dear me!

I often went to Seventy Street, whose name was later changed to "Refuse Street." The collection house where the captives were held stood in this street. Every night they would bring children for deposit into that house. It was a big, wide house with straw spread on the ground on which children, youths, and the elderly all floundered. There were iron bars on the windows of the house facing the road, and there were two guards in the reception room.

I peered through the window lattice and my heart melted like wax at what I saw. Infants shouted, "Daddy! Mommy!" Old people sat on the ground with bent heads reciting *tehillim* (Psalms) in tears, as two unruly guards with eyes dulled by drink insulted them. As I took this all in, my little brain felt overloaded because I could not comprehend: how could Jews be so cruel to one another?

I had gotten used to seeing policemen beating Jews, a landowner or soldier pinching a Jew's cheeks or spitting in his face. I had seen the Clerk of the Quarter angry with a certain powerful rich Jew when they met at the *beit midrash* (house of study), and that rich and powerful man had squirmed and pleaded like a lowly worm. Time and again I had witnessed the scorn and turpitude, blows and disgrace from the *goyim* (non-Jews), which was the lot of my Jewish brethren. It did not surprise me, because nothing I had seen in life contradicted by a single jot what is written in *Ein Yaakov:*[117] that in this world among the goyim the Jew must expect to be robbed of his good reputation, beaten and disgraced. But for Jews' hearts to harden against other Jews, that Jews could be cruel to other Jews and even laugh at their distress — I had not seen or imagined that this could happen.

One night, I woke from sleep to the sound of great tumult and scream-ing in the house. I opened my eyes and saw a battle being waged. There were disorderly and noisy strangers in the house. My father and mother were shouting at them, my sisters were howling, and the servant was cry-ing. It was a scene of chaos. I jumped out of bed in my nightshirt — the chappers were in the house! They had come to take Reb Feyvish.

My father was arguing heatedly with them, and one told him, "My advice to you, Reb Baruch, is to leave the house and let us do what we must, otherwise your end will be bitter, I warn you!" My father replied angrily, "Whatever happens, I shall not move and you shall not take the man hiding under my roof!" My mother stationed herself next to the room where Reb Feyvish was hiding and shouted: "Kill, kill Rabbi Kavrina'ar's daughter, but I will not move from here!"

One of the chappers pointed at me and said, "If you do not step aside, we will take your only son!" My mother was shocked and hid me in her arms. My father berated them and continued shouting. My sisters and the servant were wailing, and the neighbors who had gathered screamed curs-es and reprimands until the human-faced beasts relented. Eventually, the chappers left the house, saying they would soon return with the police.

My father hurriedly smuggled Reb Feyvish through gardens and courtyards to a new hiding place. The chappers did not return that night.

The next day, my father went to the head of the Kahal and had stern words with him. When he came back, he advised me not to wander the streets, quoting from the Talmud, "There is a plague in the town, remain at home," (Babylonian Talmud, Bava Kama 60B).

What I saw daily on the street from the safety of my father's house broke my heart into fragments — the torture of young children like aban-doned lambs at the hands of their drunk "uncles." My stomach turned even more during the frigid winter, seeing the infants with purple faces, shivering with cold. My heart roared and I cursed the evil people respon-sible for what had been done to these tender souls.

Israel Itzkovich:
The Story of an Archangelsk Cantonist Soldier

This chapter comes from the autobiographical account of Israel Itzkovich, a soldier of the Archangelsk Battalion. It is adapted from his published memoirs, Reminiscences of a Cantonist From Archangelsk.[118]

Israel Itzkovich came from a prosperous family. His grandfather leased many acres from landowners in the Disna District near the village of Drui. He had a distillery and floated his grain to Riga on his own barges. But in 1851–1852, the barges carrying the grain sank in an accident on the river. To make matters worse, the distillery burned down. In an instant, the Itzkovich family went from prosperity to poverty.

In 1853, when Itzkovich was seven, his family moved to the city of Polotzk in the Vitebsk District. They somehow managed to support themselves. Israel's mother sent his twelve-year-old brother to live somewhere safe from the draft. Israel and his nine-year-old sister remained at home with their mother.

One October morning, three Jewish chappers burst into their apartment, tied Israel up and carried him off. His mother's cries and screams fell on deaf ears. Itzkovich was taken to a house holding several dozen captive children. The chappers kept them there for a couple of weeks. Itzkovich's mother and relatives visited him often. They instructed him not to tell the chappers his real name, hoping that this might help him evade capture someday should he manage to escape. In any case Jews had no birth certificates at that time, and chappers would catch the first boy who came along without asking for identifying details.

About three weeks later, on October 23, 1853, the children were hauled to the receiving station where their hair was cut. When they asked Itzkovich his name, he answered "Israel-Leib," rather than reveal his real name, Elye-Leib. He claimed he did not know his last name. He gave his father's correct name: Itzko. And so the boy was listed as "Israel Itzkovich." Itzkovich spent twenty years as a Cantonist and in regular service under this name.

Itzkovich and the few dozen boys who had been inducted into the service with him were handed over to an army commander. They were housed temporarily in a barracks and issued military garments: underwear made of coarse sackcloth, overcoats, sheepskin coats and boots — none of it the right size — and a cloth knapsack in which to store their belongings

Itzkovich's service record said the following: "In view of the hiding of Jews to avoid the recruitment obligation, Israel Itzkovich, being twelve years old [they added five years], on October 23, 1853, by reason of his being underage, is being dispatched to the Archangelsk half-battalion of Cantonist soldiers."

On November 6, Itzkovich, with a detachment of boys, was sent off to the battalion. Six or more boys were placed in each of a long line of carts. Many of the Cantonists said goodbye to their families forever that day. The entire town came to bid the children farewell. The children and adults cried and screamed. The crescendo of voices shook the ground. Even after traveling several miles, Itzkovich and his companions still heard their relatives' cries.

The wagons traveled until evening when the boys arrived at a village and were assigned to quarters in cold houses with dirt floors. The children were frozen and their hands and feet were stiff with cold. A boy could not remove his knapsack because he could not unfasten the cloth buttons. If the boys cried, the diadke would fly into a rage and beat them. Several of the boys took sick and died before they arrived at their next destination, Petersburg.

From Petersburg, Itzkovich and his detachment were forcibly marched to the Siberian city of Archangelsk. This march lasted from November 1853 to June 1854. En route, the children were beaten and harassed and they died like flies. The road was littered with their corpses.

Finally, in late May or early June 1854, they entered the "Promised Land," the city of Archangelsk. The officers took the boys to a building occupied by other Cantonists.

Life for Itzkovich and his unit was full of torture and suffering. Beatings and pressure to accept baptism occurred throughout the day. Even after Itzkovich contracted an eye disease, a non-commissioned officer[119] beat him with his fists.

The officer in charge of Itzkovich and his detachment was a non-commissioned officer, a converted Jew named Yevgraf Vasilyevich Gulevich, who was the godson of the battalion commander, Dyakonov. At the first inspection of the detachment, Dyakonov declared to the battalion that as long as he lived, no one would leave his battalion a Jew. Gulevich worked to fulfill this wish of his godfather.

Every evening at about nine o'clock, when it was time for bed, Gulevich would lie down on his bed, call a few boys over and order them to kneel beside the bed. Then he would attempt to persuade the boys with quotations from the Bible, implying that the Jews were in error and that Jesus was the true savior. Finally, he would demand in a threatening tone that the boys give their consent to be converted to Christianity or else face punishment. Gulevich allowed those boys who agreed to baptism to go to sleep. The next day, they were given new uniforms and an extra piece of bread. The obstinate ones, however, were kept on their knees by his bed all night, and the next day they went without bread and were harassed and whipped on any pretext.

The older Cantonists, between the ages of twelve and fifteen, were tortured for longer durations. They were beaten and whipped so severely that many of them died of their wounds. Under these conditions, the boys, understandably, found it impossible to resist for long. They finally consented, albeit against their wishes, to accept conversion.

Every year on October 1, the Christian Holy Day of the Shroud, the Cantonists were served festive food, meaning that there were no rotten crawfish in their cabbage soup and they received one white roll each. But on the Holy Day of the Shroud in 1854, when the thousand Cantonists of the half-battalion gathered for religious services in a cramped and stuffy hall, the commander of the Second Company, Captain Garimskiy-Giro, thought he heard someone whispering. After the service, the Captain ordered that all exits be closed and the birches brought in. He had the entire company whipped until almost midnight.

Even after their forcible conversion to Christianity, Itzkovich and his fellow Cantonists suffered from continued abuse. A former Jew in an argument with a Christian comrade would still hear the epithet, *"Parkhatyy Yevri!"* (disgusting Jew). Sometimes they would add, "A Jew who has been baptized is like a wolf that has been fed!" These insults, though, served a good purpose for Itzkovich. By continually reminding him of his Jewish identity, they strengthened his inner resolve to remain a Jew. He pledged to himself that he would see justice and, without allowing fear of the penalties to dissuade him, would win back the right to be a Jew.

Every year in May, the order came from Petersburg to send the Cantonists who had turned eighteen to join the regular field troops. In 1854, the boys that had reached age eighteen, including Itskovitch's detachment, were dispatched to Petersburg and there, assigned to various units.

When Itzkovich's detachment arrived in Petersburg, it participated in an imperial review in the presence of the Tsar. During the course of the usual questioning about claims, many of the Cantonists complained about the forced conversion to Christianity. This took immense courage, as it put their lives at risk. As a result, the entire unit was placed under arrest, and they were all sentenced to a harsh punishment: to run the gauntlet past three thousand men. They all would have been beaten to death had the sentence been carried out, but it was suspended after the death of Tsar Nicholas I on February 19, 1855. Nicholas's successor, Alexander, canceled the punishment for the rest of the detachment, and only those who had themselves complained were assigned to garrison battalions in Siberia.

After the complaint from that detachment, a general from Petersburg came to visit the unit in Archangelsk. He asked if it was true that they had been forced to convert to Christianity. The general listened to the replies and then left. The commander, Colonel Dyakonov, was soon summoned to Petersburg "for explanations," but he died suddenly before he could make the journey.

When the sergeant major came to announce the death of Commander Dyakonov, he ordered that the icon lamps be lighted. Everyone in the room almost broke his feet in a joyful rush to light the icon lamps. Dyakonov's burial in a hard December frost kept the boys outdoors for over two hours; they grew stiff with cold, but it was a joyous holiday.

The manifesto of Tsar Alexander II on August 26, 1856 forbade the taking of underage Jewish children to be Cantonist soldiers, and it was soon ordered that all the boys in Cantonist battalions be released and returned to their original status. However, the return to original status pertained only to Russian child soldiers. The Jewish children, having been inducted as recruits in a scheduled recruiting levy, were not eligible for return to their previous status as Jews. The directive that concerned them ordered that the older Cantonists who had reached the age of eighteen were to be assigned to serve in the regular forces, while the younger ones were enrolled in the War Department academies.

Captain Okulov was appointed to command the First Company when Dyakonov died. Life changed for the better. The food improved and the brutal beatings stopped. The members of the company, by now adults, were dispatched to central Russia for assignment to troop units. The Second Company of younger boys was assigned to the academy.

Itzkovich was really only thirteen in 1859, but because they had added five years to his age when he was inducted into the recruits, he was listed as eighteen. Upon inspection, the commanders saw that Itzkovich was no doubt much younger, but since he wanted to finish his service as quickly as possible, he assured them that he was eighteen. In 1860, Itzkovich and seventeen others received their assignments by lot. Five were assigned to the Finland forces, three to the local Archangelsk garrison, and ten, including Itzkovich, to the Grenadier Corps.

The Grenadier Corps were dispatched on foot to Moscow. It took the Cantonists about four months to march from Archangelsk to Moscow, and they arrived in December. There, Itzkovich went into the Third Grenadier Artillery Brigade. His commander turned out to be a kind man who promoted him, the following year, to be a non-commissioned officer. He was only fourteen years old at the time, but was listed as nineteen.

Itzkovich served in the brigade for ten years. His commanders insisted that he take an officer's examination, assuring him that it would lead to further promotion. As Itzkovich prepared for the exam, he recalled how often he had heard the insult, "A baptized Jew is a well-fed wolf." He reasoned that it would be even harder to bear such insults as an officer. Giving the matter some thought, Itzkovich declined to take the examination.

Itzkovich had become a Cantonist soldier in 1853 and ended his service in 1872. He continually attempted to restore his official status as a Jew. Finally, in 1872, after serving his term, Itzkovich was released on indefinite leave. He set off for his home country to see his family again.

At home in the town of Diszna, Itzkovich learned that his father and two brothers had been banished to Siberia in 1858 for trading in contraband spirits. After he had been home for about two months, Itzkovich left for Siberia to look for his father and brothers, whom he barely remembered. He found them in the city of Tomsk.

At this point, Itzkovich was motivated by two wishes. One was to be granted retirement status and the benefits that entailed. The other was that he wanted to change his official listing back from Christian to Jew.

Itzkovich reported to the authorities that he was a soldier on indefinite leave and requested retirement status. He was informed that to receive this status he would either have to serve another ten months or maintain his status of indefinite leave for an additional three years. He chose the former and enlisted in the Tomsk Province for the purpose of serving out his remaining time.

Soon he officially declared that he did not wish to be listed as a Christian, since he had been forced to convert. His new commanders threatened Itzkovich with a trial that would deprive him of his retirement rights. Despite this, he stubbornly submitted a memorandum which set forth in detail the barbarous treatment he had received as a seven-year-old child, and how he, nevertheless, had served the Tsar honestly and conscientiously for twenty years and had received several commendations. Though his earlier commanders had tortured him and given him a new Christian name, Itzkovich claimed that his current commanders could not prohibit him from petitioning for the return of what had been taken from him by force. Itzkovich asked to be put on trial so as to end his torment.

The army commander appealed to Itzkovich to drop his request, but Itzkovich stated categorically that he would no longer betray God or His people and that he would no longer attend church or go to confession. Itzkovich's memorandum was forwarded up the chain of command. Six weeks later, he received orders from the Commander of the Forces of Western Siberia. "Non-commissioned Officer Itzkovich, who has strayed from Russian Orthodoxy, is to be presented for exhortation by a priest. If he remains unrepentant, he is to be transferred to another troop unit."

The priest tried his best but could do nothing to sway Itzkovich. In response to his exhortation, Itzkovich just smiled and said that he was no longer seven years old, but twenty-six. Nor was he transferred to another unit, since his term of service had, by that time, ended.

Itzkovich retired on October 23, 1873 after serving for exactly twenty years.

Tuvia Silverman/Shkolnik:
Musician to the Tsar

Tuvia Silverman/Shkolnik (1829–1913) was a Cantonist who became a personal musician to Tsar Nicholas. After years as a Cantonist, Silverman changed his name to Shkolnik and forgot that he was a Jew. He was reminded under unusual circumstances.

Silverman told this story to his grandson, Tzvi Shkolnik, who wrote it down in 1910 in Kielce, Poland. Tzvi Shkolnik's grandson, Arthur Skolnick, sent the story to Y.I.V.O. on September 4, 1979 from the Bronx, New York.

This account was adapted with the permission of the Y.I.V.O. Archives. The original account resides in the Y.I.V.O. Archives Territorial Collection of Russia and the Soviet Union, RG 116-Russia Folder 10.

Tuvia Silverman was born in Kobrin and had a happy childhood until he was eight years old.

One Sunday night, when Tuvia had just come home from school, his mother came home from the marketplace in distress. She told her husband, "Last night, chappers took away Breindel's boy. They may come to take our Tuvia."

She kissed Tuvia and said, "May the *Ribono Shel Olam* [Master of the Universe] protect you, my child."

Outside the rain pounded down in a steady downpour, and the roads were covered with mud. Tuvia ate supper, played with his sisters, and went to bed.

During the night, Tuvia was awakened by terrified screams. His mother was wailing and tearing her hair. His father was sobbing. His sisters were terrified. Two chappers grabbed Tuvia and hurried him into his clothes. His mother wrapped a quilt around him and embraced him. "Tuvia, my dear son," she cried. "My only *Kaddish Zugger* [child who recites the mourner's prayer for deceased family members]. Why are they tearing you away from me?"

Tuvia was taken, half-asleep, to a large house where many frightened, wide-eyed children were crying, "Mama, Mama. Take me home to my Mama!" The children cried all that sleepless night. Early the next morning, Tuvia's parents and sisters came to see him. His mother brought him a bundle of clothing. She tied a small pouch around his neck and told him quietly, "My child, when you are grown and find yourself among Jews, take this to the rabbi of the city and he will explain everything to you. Remember, my Tuvia. Be a good Jew! Remain a Jew!" When she kissed him, her tears ran down Tuvia's cheeks. His father sobbed bitterly but hugged and kissed Tuvia and said, "Tuvia, my son, may the Master of the Universe guard you from all harm. Remain a Jew."

Just as his father finished speaking these words, the guards pushed all the parents out the door. Another day passed. Tuvia and the other boys were given a meager meal. Night fell and still they waited. Late that rainy night, the boys were awoken from a restless sleep and dressed in uniforms, complete with boots lined with rags. They were driven away in a wagon, the children's wails mingling with the sounds of horse's hooves.

Tuvia and his companions traveled for many days and nights. During the trip they were fed only non-kosher food and forced to speak Russian. Finally, one day in late summer, they arrived in Moscow.

The commanding officer announced, "Children, we are now in Moscow, the home of our holy Tsar." The officers gave the boys their rations of bread and sugar cubes and took them to the barracks. Tuvia and his fellow Cantonists were taken to the baths and dressed in uniforms. Then they were given food in a large mess hall.

Several days later, the officers began training the children to be soldiers and trying to convince them to accept baptism. They subjected the boys to all sorts of tortures. The officers gathered the boys in a large hall, undressed them, and spilled beans on the ground. The boys had to kneel on the beans, which was very painful and caused Tuvia and his companions to cry. If they tried to stand up, they were whipped. Many children could not withstand the pain and intimidation and agreed to immediate baptism.

After those small conquests, torture intensified for the rest of the boys. They were taken to a very hot bath where they nearly choked from the heat and smoke. Many children fainted, many agreed to baptism. Tuvia and one other boy who remained steadfast were carried away unconscious.

When Silverman awoke, a tall officer was standing next to him holding his hand. The officer asked Silverman his name as he stroked his hand. He gave him sugar cubes and asked if he wanted to stay at his home. Silverman kissed the officer's hand and cried. The next day, he was taken to the officer's home and adopted as his son.

Silverman felt at home in the officer's house. The officer's wife treated him like the son she had never had. Every week, Silverman went to the soldiers' barracks for lessons, then returned home to his new family. The other children envied the special treatment Silverman received.

Thus the weeks, months, and years passed. Silverman forgot about his early upbringing, his former home, and his Jewish heritage. He changed his name from Silverman to Shkolnik. Eventually, he fell into bad company. He would rob innocent people and bring home their wallets for his officer, who praised him highly for his efforts.

When Silverman grew older, he displayed musical talent and was taught by a music teacher to play instruments. He received a medal for his efforts and became an accomplished musician.

Shkolnik matured and became the head of a large orchestra, often playing in officers' clubs. One day, an officer delivered an official letter to Shkolnik. It contained an invitation from the Tsar to play at a special gathering in honor of his family's rise to power. The Tsar had heard of Shkolnik's reputation as a superb musician and chose him to perform with his orchestra. Shkolnik trembled in awe at the enormity of the task. He immediately called for daily rather than weekly rehearsals to prepare the orchestra for the performance.

The great day arrived. The orchestra turned out in their new uniforms. Shkolnik pinned his two medals onto his uniform. When he arrived at the event, an elderly general greeted him with, "I hope you will make us proud and please the Tsar."

Shkolnik introduced his orchestra. When he received the signal to commence, they started with a song called *Buza Tzara Charanya* (Long

Live the Tsar). As the audience began to dance, the old general cried, "All rise!" The orchestra stopped playing, the door opened, and the Tsar and his family entered.

The royal family was seated and the orchestra resumed its serenade of polkas, waltzes, and other joyful tunes. The Tsar and his family observed that Shkolnik was constantly wiping the sweat that dripped down his face. A servant of the Tsar delivered Shkolnik the message, "The Tsar and his family are very impressed with your performance and grant you permission to remove your hat while you play." This allowed him to perform more comfortably. The music continued and the guests danced throughout the evening.

The Tsar's servant arrived once more and told Shkolnik, "Put on your hat and approach the Tsar, he wants to see you." Shkolnik humbly saluted and bowed as he approached the Tsar. The Tsar noticed his uneasiness. "Calm down, my child. What is your name? How old are you?" Shkolnik replied that he was nineteen. "You are a good boy," he said. "From now on, you are the head musician of my entourage." He gave him a silver medal.

Several days later, an order arrived confirming that Shkolnik was to be taken to the Tsar's entourage.

Some time later, a rebellion broke out in Poland. Tsar Nicholas traveled to the front lines with his entourage, including Shkolnik. En route, he drank some poisoned water and he became so sick that he spent six months recovering in the hospital.

Two years later, when Shkolnik was twenty-four years old, the Polish uprising began in earnest. The Russians sent the Tsar's cousin, Prince Morayaver, to battle. Once more Shkolnik went along. After six months, they arrived in the city of Shedlitz, Poland. Shkolnik was given lodgings by the commissar of the city. He noticed that many of the townspeople dressed strangely in small hats and long coats.

One evening, Shkolnik was invited to visit in a home in the town. Shkolnik spoke only Russian and the host and his guests spoke Polish. On some instinct, they tried speaking to Shkolnik in Yiddish. When Shkolnik replied in Yiddish they were shocked and cried out in excitement, "You are a Jew! You are a Jew!" Suddenly, Shkolnik remembered that his mother had given him a pouch containing information about his origins and had told him to go to a rabbi.

Shkolnik warned his host to remain silent on the matter and to keep it a secret. The next day the host brought him an interpreter who understood Russian, so that they could converse properly. After they spoke for a while, Shkolnik realized that he must, indeed, be a Jew. Shkolnik asked whether the Jews have a Pope. "Yes," the interpreter replied, "but we call him a rabbi." Shkolnik asked to be taken to see their rabbi.

He was sent to the rabbi together with his interpreter. The door opened and an elderly Jew with a white beard entered. Shkolnik removed his hat out of respect. The rabbi smiled and told him to put his hat back on, shook Shkolnik's hand and welcomed him. They began to converse, with the interpreter translating into Yiddish. Shkolnik took out his pouch and gave it to the rabbi, who opened it with shaking fingers and began to read the letter it contained. As he read, he started to cry.

When Shkolnik saw the rabbi crying, he too began to cry. When the two of them finally stopped sobbing, the Rabbi explained that the letter contained details of his background and the account of how he had been taken from his home.

Several weeks passed. Shkolnik became a regular guest at the rabbi's house.

One evening, Shkolnik was informed that the entourage was moving on to Shidlovtza and that he should prepare for travel. He ran to take his leave from the rabbi, who gave him a letter to deliver in person to the Shidlovtza Rebbe, one of the greatest rabbis in Poland. They bid an emotional farewell, and the rabbi blessed him. Three days later, Shkolnik departed.

The entire group of soldiers arrived in the town of Shidlovtza on a rainy, stormy night. Shidlovtza had many Jewish inhabitants. All night, the burgomaster was busy assigning the soldiers to their billets. Luckily, Shkolnik was assigned to lodge in a Jewish home. By then, he understood Yiddish with a Lithuanian accent.

Shkolnik went to call on the Shidlovtza Rebbe. When Shkolnik walked into the waiting room, dressed like a Russian soldier with a Russian-style beard, the Jews were noticeably frightened. Shkolnik asked to see the Rebbe and someone ran to call him. A middle-aged man in a *shtreimel* (fur hat worn by Hasidim for Sabbath, holidays, and special occasions) appeared, his intelligent blue eyes glowing. He leaned towards Shkolnik and Shkolnik stretched out his hand. The Rebbe ushered him in. There was dead silence in the room. The Rebbe offered Shkolnik his own chair. In broken Yiddish, Shkolnik said, *"Zetz zich, Rebbe* [please seat yourself]." Shkolnik smiled and offered the traditional greeting, "Shalom aleichem." They sat down to talk.

The Rebbe spoke to him, but Shkolnik was not sufficiently fluent in Yiddish to understand. He produced the letter from the Shedlitzer Rav. When Rebbe read it, he too started to cry. The Rebbe kissed Tuvia and laid his hand on his head to bless him. He fetched a Hasid who spoke Russian to translate, and they had a pleasant conversation. The Rebbe introduced Shkolnik to his followers and said, "This is my son Tuvia. From now on, Tuvia, you are a member of our family." The Hasidim sang and danced in Tuvia Shkolnik's honor.

They sat down to a festive meal prepared by the Rebbe's wife. Shkolnik noticed the intelligent young girl who served them. The Rabbi introduced them to each other, "This is my niece, Chana Esther; this is Tuvia, a holy Jew." He told Shkolnik that she was an orphan whom he was raising as his own child. Shkolnik was attracted to Chana Esther but dared not look at her.

Over the next several months of frequent visits, the Rebbe taught Shkolnik to pray. He became like a member of the family. On one occasion the rebbe said, "My son Tuvia, you are a great *tzaddik* (righteous individual) because though you suffered so much you have remained a Jew. You are a greater tzaddik than I. You, Tuvia, are the bridegroom for Chana Esther. May it be with *mazal* [luck]."

Shkolnik was stunned, but the Rebbe reassured him, "Don't call me Rebbe. Call me *mechutan* [father-in-law]." He called for the *shammes* [sexton], his wife and the bride. The rabbi's wife and the bride arrived dressed in their finest. The Rebbe told his niece, "You are now betrothed to Tuvia." The Hasidim drank a *l'chaim* [toast] and celebrated. Shkolnik gave his bride generous gifts of money and jewelry, and the Rebbe was pleased.

The engagement passed quickly. The Rebbe performed the wedding ceremony, and the Hasidim danced in joy.

Chana Esther and Tuvia lived happily. Their son Velvel was born a year later. Chana Esther later gave birth to another son and daughter, but unfortunately both died.

The Polish uprising was raging, and it was dangerous to be a soldier in the Tsar's army. Rebels might shoot soldiers at any time. Noblemen were hanged on any pretext. One day, Shkolnik received a letter signed by Prince Moravia, requesting the presence of his orchestra in the marketplace. When they arrived, they found a hangman's noose ready. Uncertain, they began to play. Soon the Prince arrived, then a chariot with golden wheels. There were two hangings that day: an old bishop[120] of Poland and another man who had displeased the Prince. Both were hanged before the stunned eyes of the crowd.

Some time later during this period of upheaval, Shkolnik was kidnapped by Polish rebels, who held him in an abandoned stable outside the town. They interrogated Shkolnik under torture to get him to divulge army intelligence. Shkolnik held out and refused to give away any sensitive information.

Someone found Shkolnik's lost hat and took it to Chana Esther. Certain that he was dead, she sat *shiva* (the traditional seven-day mourning period) for him.

Late one night, Shkolnik heard someone call him, then break through the wooden door of the stable.

"Tuvia, I am a Jew from your town," he said. "I have come to save you." He untied Shkolnik, and Tuvia fled to his home and knocked at the door.

"Who's there?" asked Chana Esther.

"Tuvia," he replied.

Assuming he was dead and returning to haunt her, she cried out, "Go to your eternal rest!"

Tuvia protested that he was still very much alive. Terrified, Chana Esther woke the shammes. The members of the community were excited to see Shkolnik safe and sound. The Prince expressed his gratitude for safeguarding confidential army intelligence and gave him a medal.

"Next week," he announced, "we are going to Kiltetz in Russia. We will be safer there."

Chana Esther was sorry to leave her family in Poland, but as Tuvia was still serving out his army service, they had to comply with the Prince's orders.

The months passed. Shkolnik completed his years of army service and opened a successful store. One day years later, a woman knocked on the door.

"Does Tuvia live here?"

His wife was cautious. "Yes. Who are you?"

"I want to see him," was all the woman would say.

Chana Esther suspected that this woman might be Tuvia's wife from a previous marriage. But she need not have worried. The woman was Shkolnik's older sister, Zlata, who had been searching for him for years. The siblings were finally reunited.

Shkolnik and his wife bought a piece of property and built a house. High Holiday services were prayed in their home with a Torah scroll from the Shedlovitza Rebbe, Nosson Dovid'l.

Thus, Tuvia Shkolnik found his way back to the Jewish people. His descendants carried on his name and his memory.

Moisy Spiegel: Twists of Fortune

Moisy Spiegel was a Cantonist. In 1911 he published his story *From the Notes of a Cantonist* in *Yevreiskaya Starina*.

Moisy Spiegel was born to a middle-class family in the region of Zaslavky Uzeyd in the province of Voleansk. His father died in 1850 when he was six, and a year later, he was kidnapped from his home when his mother was out, and turned in toward the draft quota. Spiegel's mother found out that he had been taken to Novogorod-Voleansk and managed to come up with the hefty ransom for his release.

For three months, until the end of the recruitment season, he was hidden behind a stove in the home of a Ukrainian. All that winter, Spiegel's many relatives discussed how to keep him out of harm's way. When his father had been alive, his older brother Levi had been sent away to avoid conscription to an uncle in Lemberg, Austria. After long deliberations, Spiegel's relatives decided to sell their houses and belongings and leave for Austria after the Passover holiday. Twenty-four of them joined other Jews who had gathered in Voleansk in preparation for emigration. Some Moldavians and Jews agreed, for a fee of twenty rubles per person, to get the group across the river and past the border.

The Moldavians pretended to be hauling food on their oxen, when in fact, refugees were hidden in their bushel baskets. They warned the refugees not to stand up so that they would pass the frontier guards undetected. But at about seven o'clock on a Friday night, soldiers on horses surrounded the oxen and caught them all. The next day, the children were handcuffed together in pairs, the adults were placed in irons, and the whole group was sent off, first to Kamensk-Podolzk, later to other cities until their scheduled court hearings. At the end of May, the family paid a fee that bought their release.

In 1852, when Spiegel was eight, preparations began for war with Turkey. A new round of recruitment caused great anxiety to the local Jews. During the day, people were too busy to dwell on the danger, but at night, nobody could sleep for worry. Spiegel and his mother wept every time she hugged him. Spiegel remained in hiding for some time until he was transported to his uncle in Zaslav. However, despite all efforts to avoid conscription, Spiegel was eventually caught. He was sent to the city of Ostrog and from there, in late August, to Zhitomir.

About ten days before the Jewish New Year, the child was undressed for examination by the doctor and a military officer. They casually pronounced him fit for service and sent him to the next room, where many small children were crying bitterly.

Ukrainian women offered them food from pots and tried to calm them. "Eat please, for your health," they urged the boys. The women brought food to the barracks twice a day until the group departed.

Before Spiegel's group of two hundred and twenty-five boys departed, his mother managed to find him in Zhitomir. When she arrived, Spiegel was eating Ukrainian poppy-seed and fruit pie. But it was too late — no payoff could buy his freedom this time.

The boys were fitted for official state uniforms. The single-breasted coat of gray fabric had gray cloth buttons and a standing collar with hooks. The greatcoat was long and baggy, without pockets. The brimless lined hat was ugly, too large, made from a thick fabric. The pants were a thick cloth with a rough canvas lining — they did not fit and irritated the skin with their rubbing. The boots were made of coarse leather. Since winter was approaching, the boys were also provided with poor short sheepskin coats. These were infested with fleas and lice that gave them no peace, and the constant scratching brought rashes. Spiegel carried a backpack made of peasant cloth containing two coarse shirts, a kerchief, socks, and drawers that his mother had brought him.

The boys were only allowed to keep a small amount of money. Any larger sum they might have had from home was given to an officer for "safekeeping" and never returned.

The boys slept in the barracks, packed together like fish in a barrel. The very next day Spiegel's group started their training. They were commonly addressed, "Hey you, Yids!"

One week later, about two or three days before Rosh Hashanah, the boys left Zhitomir surrounded by relatives who wept as if they were on their way to the cemetery for a burial or hanging. Fathers, mothers, brothers, and sisters followed them as long as they could, for three or four stations. Spiegel's mother's last words to him were, "My son, never betray your faith."

The children arrived at Moscow in the winter during a harsh cold spell. Their frigid barracks contained filthy bunks; their food was served from big pots similar to the barrels often used for cows' feed. Five days later, an adjutant came to conduct an audit and asked whether there were any complaints. But since the boys did not know any Russian, no one could speak out.

The boys didn't know what was planned for them, but the very next day they left Moscow on foot. They were marched to an outlying town called Hodlinka. The children were placed with families in whose homes they were constantly berated for being Jewish. Whenever they entered a room, they were greeted with, "Yids, nonbelievers!" The boys were not prepared for this sort of abuse.

The boys gathered one day on the street and decided to leave the torment and humiliation and return to Moscow. Though some of the older boys were more judicious, none of them understood the grave implications of carrying out a "rebellion."

Together, the boys went back to Moscow late at night and ended up in a town square. Their officers happened to be visiting friends in Moscow that night, and all the supervisors were out enjoying themselves in bars. The boys were rounded up by several policemen, one of whom was a Jewish soldier. They told the policemen their story.

They were transferred to a large stone building housing the Chief of Police. He felt it was a serious enough matter to bring to the attention of the Governor General, who had them fed and put to sleep, and sent a messenger to Suhozanev, the Minister of the Military. In the morning, the authorities heard the case and ordered that the children's supervisors be arrested. They appointed new officers to take charge of the boys, along with a clerk who was a Jew who had converted to Christianity.

The boys' fate had fortunately, for the time being, fallen into the hands of humane individuals. They were taken to Nijniy-Novogorod. On the road they were fed well, especially when they were billeted in wealthy households. Still, many of the boys could not tolerate the pork they were fed and had stomachaches, fevers and rashes. The boys were plagued by the bugs that infested their clothing and washed only occasionally in public bathhouses.

After Passover, the children arrived at Nijniy-Novogorod where the Russian townspeople accepted them with great hospitality.

They stayed in Nijniy for three days and were seen off with wishes for good health and a safe trip in a pompous ceremony in the market square. Two merchants gave each boy fifty kopecks, a bar of soap, a loaf of white bread, a white shirt and a red, a towel, two kerchiefs, a pair of boots, a brush, needles and thread. Equipped with these belongings, they set off for the next stage of their service.

The children learned fluent Russian during their long journey to the Siberian city of Tobolsk. One hundred and ten boys commenced the journey together, but some fell ill during the trip and were left in hospitals along the way. A few of them were dying when they were left behind.

The boys lived a Spartan life of rigid military routine. The duty officer and supervisor of the Cantonists would wake the children at six o'clock every morning. They were allowed to wash their faces, brush their teeth with charcoal powder and to perform minimal ablutions in a sink in the supervisor's room. Each Cantonist had to make his bed to military specifications. Then they cleaned their jackets and tights, polished their black boots, and dressed. They lined up to sing Christian hymns, "Our Father" and "Rise Up." Each boy received a quarter pound of black bread and salt. In the winter, they received candles but no kerosene for heat.

They were forbidden to speak Yiddish among themselves, but continued to do so secretly. The boys were also forbidden to recite Jewish prayers silently or to celebrate Jewish holidays. Spiegel and his comrades tried secretly to find out anything they could from the Siberian Jewish children among them. Though local, their parents were forbidden to visit.

The regiment was demanding and there was little allowance for failure. Spiegel and his group were disciplined with an iron fist. Each group of ten boys was supervised by a teacher who was himself a Cantonist. That winter, they trained twice daily. They had to march in the correct manner and stand motionless while they were given their orders. The boys practiced posture and had to raise one leg slowly and stand firmly on the other leg. Weak children fell like sheaves of straw. The officer and the non-commissioned officer observed the practice sessions.

The boys were kept in line with harsh threats, and a careless student faced various punishments. The children's ribs, sides and chins were squeezed until they dissolved in tears. If a boy moved when he was supposed to stand still, he had to kneel and hold a heavy wooden box of sand for the rest of the day without any dinner. Boys were assigned to help the soldier-cooks in the kitchen to peel potatoes and carry wood to the stoves, or to help the bread-makers bake bread. A boy might be assigned to help in the office, carry military packages and clean or stoke the stoves in the office, help the bathhouse attendant, or clean a large yard. Besides these assignments, if a Cantonist did not do his homework, he had to clean the classroom floors with sawdust and he would go home with one of the teachers to clean his house and do his chores. At night, the teacher had to report to the superintendent whether the assignments performed by the Cantonist had been carried out to his satisfaction.

Besides military training, classes were held in the five-classroom building next to the barrack. In one classroom, five groups of ten Cantonist students would form half circles. The teacher (a Cantonist himself) stood in the middle of the group with a pointer.

After passing an entrance exam, the student was placed in the lower second grade. If he did not perform well, he was expelled and sent to a workshop. In the second and third grades, a Cantonist studied compound numbers, simple and decimal fractions, geometry, geography, intermediate grammar, drawing, Russian history, religious studies, orthography, military accounting, and service regulations, among other subjects.

Spiegel passed the entrance exam in 1854 and was placed in the lower second grade. On Mondays and Thursdays, at drawing classes, the teacher would sternly reprove, "You, Yid, do not want to learn how to draw icons!" He "rewarded" Spiegel for his drawings with hard smacks on the hand with the edge of a ruler.

Spiegel was once sent to the hospital with swollen hands from this treatment. While there, more experienced Cantonists helped him extend his stay in the hospital by teaching him to scrub his eyes with an irritant to give the appearance of sickness. The medical attendant, himself a converted Jew, cooperated with the ruse by agreeing not to apply the prescribed medicine for Spiegel's eyes. Spiegel spent a month in the hospital, which was a welcome relief, though he had to make up his missed studies.

The officers, including the teacher Captain Shuhov, attempted to coerce baptism, though they were rewarded for reporting that the boys' acceptance of Russian Orthodoxy had been voluntary. In Spiegel's group of one hundred and ten Jewish boys, only thirty to forty boys remained who had not converted to Christianity. Every day they were punished for their stubbornness. Meanwhile, the boys were taught daily to pray in Russian, and they had to attend church weekly. Nobody protested this pressure to convert. Even the parents of the Siberian Jewish children were afraid to interfere for fear of harsher punishment.

The priest who worked with the Cantonists, Father Bogolub, was delighted when Spiegel answered his questions with a reference from the New Testament, such as "Our Father." Bogolub often took Spiegel to his home to play with his children.[121] His wife and daughters fed Spiegel and wheedled him to cross himself. Often, they hung a cross around his neck and assured him that Christ was himself a Jew.

The pressure to convert never ceased, even when masked in kindness. Spiegel sometimes appeared to waver, but his mother's parting words gave him strength. Spiegel was hated for his stubbornness; Bogolub concluded that it was impossible to convert Spiegel.

When the Manifesto of Alexander was issued in 1856, the number of officer-teachers working with the Cantonists was reduced. Captain Shuhov and a few others remained. About one hundred fifty Jewish children remained on the military campus but were released from rigorous military training, with classes and maneuvers canceled that summer. Only workshops and marching practice continued. The boys were treated differently: allowances were increased from one and a half to eight kopecks a month, the daily beatings stopped, and the boys were allowed to go to town and visit friends.

In the third grade, Spiegel's marks were excellent and he was sometimes left in charge of the class. Spiegel often assisted with the children of General Dometti, dining and sleeping with them. Conditions had clearly changed for the better.

The 1856 Manifesto of Alexander II marked the end of the Cantonist system, but not all its provisos were shared with the Cantonists themselves.

In 1858, when Spiegel was fourteen and was in training to be a clerk, he and two of his friends were accepted into the base headquarters office for on-the-job training in preparation for the Ministry of the Military exam. This was their last exam before Spiegel was scheduled to graduate in 1859 and become a clerk with the rank of non-commissioned officer.

One day, when their supervisor Pritchin left the office, he forgot to lock the cabinet containing a carefully guarded box. The boys decided to find out what the mysterious box contained. In it they discovered secret documents from the Chief of Military Institutions, General-Adjutant Annenkov. One forbade the army to force Jewish child-Cantonists to accept Christianity. Nonetheless, the pressure to coerce Spiegel continued. So much for the official rules!

Chaim Merimzon:
The Story of an Old Soldier

This life story is adapted from the recollections of Chaim Merimzon, published in several installments in *Yevreiskaya Starina* as 'Razkaz Storago Soldata' (The Story of an Old Soldier) in 1913–1914.[122]

A Birthday to Remember

Late afternoon on the Sabbath eve of Chaim Merimzon's eleventh birthday, his family was preparing for a joyous Sabbath of celebration. Chaim's parents had purchased the honor for Chaim of reading the *haftorah* (a chapter of the Prophets) in the synagogue on Sabbath morning. His father, Yosef, a *melamed* (teacher of Jewish subjects), had listened to Chaim read the portion and was confident that he would perform well and bring pride to his parents. His mother, Merele, had baked cakes for a party while Merimzon and his father went together to the mikva. When they returned, Merimzon's father had sent him on one last errand before the Sabbath: to bring some vodka from the local tavern.

Chaim ran toward the tavern, too excited to walk. His mind was full of the upcoming festivities. "What a wonderful Sabbath we will have! My father and my teacher Reuven will pour me a small glass of vodka and we will all toast, "L'chaim!" Mama and her friend Chava will cut me a big slice of cake. I will dunk the cake in my vodka and we will all sing Sabbath songs. Oh, what a fine time we will have!"

When Merimzon turned into Varshavskaya Street, he saw a large, enclosed wagon with a pair of horses. Two middle-aged Jews were sitting in the wagon and the driver was a young Lithuanian. One of the Jews called to Merimzon and asked where the tavern was.

"Down at the very end of this street," he answered. "I'm on my way there now."

"Climb up onto the wagon and we'll take you there," they offered.

The moment Merimzon had taken his seat, the Jews said something to the driver in Lithuanian. He whipped the horses, and the team took off in a cloud of dust. When they reached the tavern, Merimzon told them, "Stop here!" but they kept going and drove deep into the forest. The sun was already setting. The driver stopped and the Jews climbed down to recite the Mincha afternoon prayers.

Kidnap

Merimzon began to scream and cry when he realized that the Jews were chappers. He tried to bolt, but the driver held him in a firm grip until the "pious ones" had finished their prayers. They climbed back onto the wagon and restrained Merimzon by force. They drove through the forest on winding roads until they drew up in front of a hut.

Sabbath candles were already burning on the table. A little boy was huddled, sobbing, in the corner. They invited him to the table to pray and celebrate the Sabbath day, but he refused. At first Merimzon, thought that he was a son misbehaving, but he soon realized that the boy was also a captive. They seated Merimzon at the table and gave him a Sabbath prayer book. Merimzon felt like crying himself, but he remembered that his father had told him that it is a sin to cry on the Sabbath. So he prayed in a clear voice, singing the usual Sabbath melodies. When he reached L'cha Dodi (the Friday night prayer welcoming the Sabbath), he tried to trill like the cantor.

"Such a good boy!" they exclaimed over him. The mistress of the house kissed him, but Merimzon thought to himself: "May the Angel of Death kiss you!"

The chappers chanted the Sabbath evening prayers, swaying back and forth.

The two chappers sat down at the table with the master and mistress of the house and tried again to get the crying boy to join them. One of the chappers attempted to drag him to the table by the arms, but the boy was stubborn and he grabbed the man by his beard, like a crawfish.

"Leave him alone, the stubborn *shaygetz* [non-Jew, here a 'ruffian']!" said the others. "We'll call the driver to take him into the woods for the wolves to eat." The poor little fellow was left with nothing to eat. He kept trying to escape, but they guarded him carefully. Merimzon, on the other hand, observed the usual Sabbath rituals.

The table was elaborately set. In the middle were the burning Sabbath candles and a large bottle of vodka surrounded by glasses. A plump challah lay next to each plate and two, covered with a snow-white napkin, lay at the host's place. The host chanted the *Kiddush* (ritual blessing over the wine on the Sabbath) and drank. They served Merimzon his own glass, and after reciting the Kiddush clearly, he tossed it down in one gulp. The group performed the ritual washing of the hands and sliced the challahs.

When the host suggested singing the Sabbath songs, the chappers refused, since they were worn out from their trip and their hunting expedition. However, they could not refuse to chant the grace after the meal, so when the host offered the chapper who was a *Cohen* (a descendant of the Biblical Aaron, therefore a member of the priestly caste) the honor of the grace, he splashed his fingertips with water and uttered the opening line, "Esteemed friends! Let us bless!" Everyone responded in unison and then mumbled the prayer quickly, since they wanted to get to sleep.

After supper, they put their two young prisoners into a dark little room with one window and bolted the door from the outside. The little boy wouldn't stop crying.

"Stop crying, silly," Merimzon told him. "After all, it's the Sabbath, and it is a sin to cry on the Sabbath."

"This is a fine Sabbath for you," the boy said angrily, sniffling. "You sat there with those robbers, gorging yourself like a pig. You have nothing to cry about, but I do."

"And just who told you not to eat? They even tried to drag you to the table, but you were too stubborn."

"Ah, brother," the sobbing child replied, "I see that you are a blockhead. Do you know where they are taking us? They are going to drive us deep into the heart of Russia and give us to the filthy Great Russians, who will make us eat pork and force us to make the sign of the cross. How will you like that?"

"Even supposing you're right, will our tears really do any good? And whom will it bother if you don't eat? No, little brother, tears can't set things right. As long as your soul is in your body, you have to eat and drink what God gives you. I advise you to sit at the table tomorrow and eat. There will be plenty of time to cry later if God doesn't have mercy on us."

Early the next morning, Machek, the driver, opened the shutters and the door and ordered the boys to wash up. The mistress of the house brought the boys a prayer book and Merimzon convinced his comrade in misfortune not to cry. The boys prayed fervently alongside their hosts in their prayer shawls. When they had finished, they all sat down to lunch.

The host gave each of them a little glass and asked Merimzon's companion, "What's your name, boy?"

"Yankel [Yiddish diminutive of Yaacov, Hebrew for Jacob]."

"And your family name?"

"Klezmer [literally, a Jewish folk musician]."

"You have a lively name, yet you cry," the host observed sarcastically.

Merimzon drank his glass of vodka as he had the day before, but Yankel would not drink, no matter how hard the host and the kidnappers tried to convince him.

Merimzon asked Klezmer, "Did you sing the Sabbath songs at home?"

"Yes."

"But, after all, it is said: 'God said to Jacob: Be not afraid, My servant Jacob.' You and I must have hope, too. No matter where they take us, God is everywhere. And it might happen that we shall meet people who want us to take on an alien faith or to destroy us in some other way, but the tears of our parents will fall on their heads. And I have also heard it said that payment for sin is meted out justly, 'measure for measure.'"

Yankel listened and thought, then took his glass, said the blessing, and toasted, "L'chaim." The chappers left the table, unable to eat with the boys; they asked the hostess to feed the boys their *kugel* first and let them eat with the host later.

"Ach," they said, "if we could only turn them in sooner, these *mamzers* [literally illegitimate children — derogatory term]! They've eaten their way into our livers, especially this Chaimka with his biting words."

After lunch, the boys asked to walk in the woods, hoping to evade their captors. But the chappers had had victims slip out of their hands before and refused the boys' request.

The hostess took the boys into their room and said, "Children, before the evening meal, read a chapter of Psalms and ask God to give us a good week and good health." She left the room and bolted the door.

Yankel's deep sighs were constant and the tears rolled down his chubby, pale cheeks. "What is happening with my poor parents? They are probably killing themselves with sorrow, not knowing to where I have disappeared." Merimzon's heart ached and he felt like crying himself, but because of the Holy Sabbath, he maintained his composure and tried to comfort Klezmer: "Be not afraid, Jacob!"

The sun was close to setting and the boys recited the evening prayer. The hostess let them out of their cell and fed them. The kidnappers watched them closely, as did two retired soldiers they had hired to serve as guards until they sent the boys off.

It became dark, and the Sabbath was nearly over. The chappers ordered Machek the driver to prepare for the journey, while they all recited the evening prayers. The host performed *havdala* (literally 'separation'; a brief service marking the official end of the Sabbath).

The Holy Sabbath was over and it was now a regular weekday; in Chaim's mind, it was now all right to cry. Merimzon and Yankel returned to their room, and Merimzon recited a psalm: "Lord, in my distress I cry to Thee" and began to sob.

"Ach, my poor parents!" he thought. "How did they get through this Sabbath without me? I was due to chant the haftorah in the synagogue. But robbers have captured me, just as hawks snatch a chick from a hen."

The boys wailed, raising such a howl that had it happened in town, people would have taken that thieves' den apart log by log and rescued the boys. Machek took Merimzon by the arms, one of the guards grabbed Yankel, and they loaded them into the wagon.

The hosts rode along. On the way, they tried to calm the children by saying that they would plead on their behalf that they be allowed to return home. The boys stopped crying and fell asleep.

They startled awake when the wagon stopped at a tall stone building guarded by a soldier with a rifle. The chappers dusted off the boys' coats and cleaned them up with their dirty handkerchiefs, scrubbing their pale cheeks until they shone red. Then they led them up the stairs to the second floor of the building.

Welcome to the Military

An officer at the last table motioned their "guardians" to bring the boys closer. He ordered Merimzon, "State your first name and your surname." Merimzon turned to one of the chappers for a translation.

He turned back to the gentleman and said, "Chaim Merimzon."

The man looked at the paper he held and shouted, "Your name is Meyer, not Chaim! Look here, call yourself Meyer!"

Merimzon recognized the name and it dawned on him that he was being substituted for a rich tavern keeper with the same last name.

"And what is your name?" the man demanded of Klezmer.

"Yankel Klezmer."

"You're lying!" he insisted. "Your name is Itsik Grinblat."

The officer recorded the children's names and ordered their peyot cut off. He finished his business with the chappers and they departed. Escorts with rifles arrived to take Merimzon and Klezmer to the recruiting jail where they would remain until they could be assigned to troop units.

The escorts jeered and mocked the boys on the way to the jail, pushing them to walk faster. "Do you get it? Our little Jews are no fools; some are soldiers and others are crawfish." "Jew, did you hear, today is the Sabbath. How do you feel about that?" and "The Jew ate a pig's ear!"

The jail contained several rooms for recruits, where they were held separately from regular prisoners. Long plank beds, not quite two feet off the floor, ran along both walls. On the beds lay filthy mattresses made of coarse sacking stuffed with straw. Adult conscripts were sleeping on the mattresses; boys had to lay under the plank beds on the bare floor. The beds were so low that they could not even lift their heads. They couldn't sleep face up, either, because dust and bits of straw sifted down from the threadbare mattresses. The children slept this way for three weeks until the adults were sent off. When the adults left, the boys climbed up happily onto the mattresses and considered themselves lucky.

A Jewish contractor fed the boys kosher food until they were dispatched. Every day he hauled in a pot of pea or bean slops or potato soup with barley. With his copper ladle the contractor would dip out one measure into each boy's bowl. The boys ate with kosher wooden spoons. The bowls and spoons were washed every two weeks when the children were taken to the bathhouse. Adult soldiers were allotted three pounds of bread, but since the Cantonists were underage, they received only two pounds. The boys were allowed as much meat as they could consume at one sitting per week. Members of the local community donated challahs on the Sabbath for the contractor to dole out equally. Since merchants were kept away from the boys, this was the limit of their food supply.

Merimzon's father, Yosef, tried to see his son when he found out that he was in this military school. Since he was a teacher and did not know military procedures, he walked straight up to the gates of the jail as if he were going to the beit midrash. The sentry struck the Jew with a rifle butt for daring to approach in this way. Merimzon's father fell and lay unconscious for some time. Some Jews came running over to revive him and carry him to the Jewish hospital. He was held in jail for six weeks after his release from the hospital, during which time he heard that his son and the other boys had been fitted with uniforms and sent away to the Kiev Cantonist Battalions.

Journey to the Kiev Battalion

A Jewish carrier of goods and freight received the contract to provide the big, high carts on which the recruits were to be transported. Sixteen boys were squeezed into each cart like sardines. Merimzon and his friend "Grinblat" tried to stick together. Their bond helped them struggle together to survive. They shared every bite of their rations and, together, recited prayers and psalms.

The boys tried to keep each other's spirits up. They reminisced about their old lives and how they used to play at home. They sang together to escape their new reality; some would mimic improvisation of verses at weddings in their native towns.

Often, the Cantonists speculated on the fate that awaited them.

"I heard," said Grinblat, "that where they are taking us, they make you get baptized; when someone is stubborn, they torture him; but when someone agrees, they teach him military science until he is eighteen or twenty years old and then make him an officer.... No, I will not do that. They should live so long, that I should sell out my holy faith to be an officer! No, I would let my body be cut into pieces first.... Let them kill me."

The journey dragged on for three months. The Cantonists rode in the tall carts with a large detachment of convoy troops following on foot. The troops had been charged with strict vigilance in looking after the boys as if they were desperate convicts.

At that time, foot travelers walked for two days and rested on the third. Every third day, the children were stationed in peasants' huts, unless they had reached a town or city where there was a barracks or jail to hold them while more recruits were rounded up for deportation.

The boys did not bathe for the duration of the journey. As a result, vermin — fleas and lice — multiplied in their clothing and underwear. The children felt that their bodies were covered with stinging nettles. When it became unbearable, they burst into tears. Their escorts rushed them like wild beasts, shouting, "Why are you raising such a fuss, you damned Jewish babies?" They cursed the boys and threatened them with their fists. The boys were struck dumb with fear, but their tears continued to pour silently down their cheeks.

The children were heartsick when the convoy approached Kiev. Judgment Day was coming. Their escorts shouted out, "Climb out, Jewish babies!" The boys took up their little bags and climbed out of the carts. The escort soldiers arranged them in ranks and led them into the city.

Merimzon looked around this large city. It was vast and looked endless, unlike his little town, which was entirely visible from any vantage spot. In Kiev he saw many large, beautiful churches with tall bell towers. Merimzon look down the streets for a synagogue, but he saw none.

The children were marched through the marketplace. The people were tall with broad shoulders and rosy cheeks. They walked briskly back and forth and conversed loudly in a strange language. It struck Merimzon as quite different from the manner in which the gaunt, bent Jews carried themselves in his town, murmuring to each other, gasping and coughing. He saw stout, buxom market women with broad faces, hawking their wares from large baskets of sweets and fruits. They called to each other in ringing, merry voices. When the children passed them, they called to them mockingly, "Hey, little Jews, buy something from us — some vegetables and horseradish for the Sabbath!"

The escort marched the boys to the barracks. Cantonist troops from the Polish provinces arrived that same day. The escort troops lined them up in long rows in three ranks, instructing them, "When the commander says, 'Hello, boys!' answer loudly, 'We wish you good health, your honor!'"

Soldiers carried bundles of birch rods past them. When Merimzon saw the birches, his heart sank and a chill pierced his body. The children stood like shadows, and a deathly silence fell over the group. A prayer echoed in Merimzon's soul, "Our patroness, mother Rachel, rise from your grave and ask our Almighty God, who will accept your tears, to send His guardian angel to protect us from all misfortunes, and to give us the energy and the strength to remain loyal to our holy faith!"

The senior escort, seeing the commander approaching, called out, "Attention! Eyes right! Listen, you Jewish babies; answer as I told you!"

Fear gripped Merimzon. "How will we be able to pronounce such a long greeting correctly, in this language we don't understand? After all, he said it only once.... Why didn't he teach it to us on the way? Can we really say it right from that one example, 'We wish you good health, your honor?' And if we don't answer correctly, the commander will order them to whip us.... They've already brought out the birches. We won't get by without a whipping today!"

The commander drove up, stopped at the center of the front line, surveyed the boys and shouted with a smile, "Hello, children!" They responded in unison, sounding like goats, "Meeeeh!," but they must have done a passable job because the birches did not appear. Sergeant majors with company clerks divided the boys into companies by height. Merimzon was sent to the Fifth Company and his friend Grinblat to the Fourth. Finally, they went to the bathhouse.

Army Life and Billets

The boys did not stay in the Cantonist barracks for long, but were sent to the Chernigov Province. They were assigned to two districts, Nezhinskiy and Novozybkovskiy, where they were quartered in private village homes. At that time, the whole Novozybkovskiy District was Old Believer[123] territory, including the home where Merimzon was billeted.

His landlady led him to a dark corner behind the stove, where a sack of straw lay on the floor. This, she indicated, was his bedroom.

Merimzon was thirsty and scooped some water from the water bucket with a ladle. He was about to drink when the landlady threw herself at him like an enraged lioness. She struck him and screamed, "Anti-Christ! Foul Satan!" Merimzon was dumbfounded, but could not ask her why she cursed him since he did not speak Russian. The landlady shoved him in the chest to get him away from her sacred water bucket. Merimzon wanted to hit her back, but was afraid that they would whip him for it. He resolved to ask a more experienced Cantonist about the customs of the Christians to avoid such scenes in the future.

In the evening, Merimzon went to bed in his dark corner without any supper. He used his little bag as a pillow and covered himself with his overcoat. He tossed and turned for a long time, thinking of his mother and how she had always sung him lullabies. But he could not fall asleep; he was hungry, and lice, fleas, and bedbugs were biting his flesh. Finally, he cried himself to sleep.

In the morning, the landlady served Merimzon a slice of bread, a bit of lard and a pinch of salt. She said something in a kind tone, pointing to the edge of the stove. He guessed that this was to be his table. He ate the bread and salt and fed the lard to the cat.

Merimzon heard a drummer calling the boys, so he dressed and ran to assembly. The children lined up outside the village. The company commander shouted, "Whoever wants to be baptized — step forward!" Birch rods were displayed prominently as inducement. Many were frightened and stepped forward immediately, but Merimzon felt his responsibility, as the son of a Torah instructor and the grandson of a rabbi, to remain true to his faith at any cost. If worse came to worst, he was prepared to die by his own hand to sanctify God's name.

Punishment followed. The children who did not step forward were beaten. The officers jeered at the boys, taunted and tortured them. They singled Merimzon out for harassment because they blamed him for the resistance of the others to baptism. They thought that if Merimzon agreed to convert, the others would follow suit. They continually tried to wear down his resolve.

Merimzon did his best to live by his principles, though survival required some concessions. At first, he could not bear to taste the bread with lard that was all his landlady gave him to eat. When he was hungry enough to put a spoonful of the lard into his mouth, his kosher stomach regurgitated it immediately. For three months, Merimzon lived on bread and water until he realized that he would not survive on such a diet. With great difficulty, Merimzon accustomed his stomach to the food that was so offensive to him.

Cantonist training centered on memorizing Russian Orthodox prayers and military terminology. The boys were expected to know the appropriate form of address for all ranks, from the Tsar to a lance corporal. Merimzon was resourceful, and he hired his teacher to tutor him privately, paying him with sunflower seeds or a couple of rolls. The teacher dictated the material to be memorized and Merimzon recorded it in Hebrew letters. He would study his notations all evening, then go confidently to the next morning's training session. The corporal would ask questions and Merimzon was quite sure he knew the answers. But he soon found out that his plan was flawed, and was punished for mispronouncing words. For example, instead of *"Otche nash, izhe osi"* (Our Father, who art...), Merimzon would say, *"Otse nas, ize oshi."* The Hebrew alphabet has no exact letters for transliterating the Russian sounds *shch, zh* or *y*. Merimzon could not pronounce the letter y at all, and he said *"mi"* instead of *"my."* So Merimzon, together with all the other Cantonists, had to present his palm for caning. The boys returned from training sessions with swollen palms and eyes red from crying.

A different kind of hell plagued the boys in their quarters: harassment by the children of the families with whom they lived. The children were ingenious in inventing ways to taunt the Cantonists. They chalked crosses on their overcoats and smeared their mouths with lard. One day, Merimzon gathered his courage, and when his landlady's son rushed him with the lard he planned to smear on his lips, Merimzon hit him in the nose with a handy implement and bloodied his nose. The mistress of the house threw herself on Merimzon like an enraged tigress; if he had not run away, she would have torn him to shreds.

She pursued Merimzon screaming, "Guard! The Jew has killed my Petka!" People gathered, the Cantonists and non-commissioned officers were assembled, and the drummer beat the alarm. Merimzon grabbed an iron shovel, braced himself in a defensive position against a wall, and silently prayed, *"L'yeshuascha kivisi Hashem* [I set my hope in your salvation, God]."

The officers ordered Merimzon to drop the shovel, and they took him to the company commander. On the way, he silently recited the Twentieth Psalm of David.[124] The commander questioned Merimzon. Though he still could not quite understand what he was being asked, Merimzon had learned enough to produce the appropriate soldiers' responses and barked out "Yes, sir, your honor!" "At your service, your honor!" and "Very good, sir!" in response to the questions he was asked. The commander ordered Merimzon moved to different quarters. To placate the landlady, he promised that he would order Merimzon whipped.

Turning Point

Merimzon's prayers were answered and the new quarters turned out to be a vast improvement. The master and mistress of the house had no children to harass him. The landlord was a kind man. With an ardent prayer of thanks to God for His goodness, Merimzon slept.

When the kind landlady gave him breakfast and took him to training, Merimzon was reminded of walking with his mother to school. He thanked God for helping him escape his difficult former quarters. "Now I will only have to suffer in training...." But things improved there too. He was promoted to the rank of private, and during the year, learned fluent Russian. He mastered the material in his courses and the beatings ended. He would go off to training cheerfully, with his service cap at a jaunty angle.

At the beginning of his conscription, Merimzon received a monthly letter containing one ruble from his parents. After a year, the letters stopped suddenly. Merimzon wrote many letters, but received no answer. "God knows whether they are alive. How can I find out?" he asked himself. The question preoccupied him, and one day when he was too depressed to eat, his kind landlady noticed that something was wrong.

"Why are you so sad, little soldier? Did they beat you?"

"No, auntie, I'm sad because I have not heard from my parents in almost six months.... I don't even know whether they are still alive."

"Send them a letter," She advised.

"I have written several times already, but I received no answer."

"Then write to some friend or to your rabbi, who will be sure to answer."

Merimzon sent a letter to his former teacher, Reuven. He waited for weeks and finally received a letter with a ruble. Merimzon was overjoyed, but his joy turned to sorrow when he read the letter:

> Our former son, Chaim (but the devil knows what to call you now — Ivan or something else),
>
> We are sending you a ruble; buy yourself some rope and hang yourself, or tie a stone around your neck and drown yourself. Be damned henceforth and forever more. Forget our names. Do not send us your false letters. We will not accept them from the postman. Now you have new parents; let them give you rubles.
>
> If we die before you, we will not be silent in the next world but will curse you and will never give you peace. You have sullied our names and the name of your grandfather, which you bear. You have brought shame on our family name, you villain. Because of you, street urchins run after us shouting, "Your Chaimka is a *meshumed* [an apostate who voluntarily abandoned Judaism]!" A meshumed! If what we have been told is not true, send us certification from a rabbi that you have not converted to Christianity. Then you will remain our beloved son.

Merimzon assumed that his parents had been driven mad by grief and sadness. His father, evidently, was not in his right mind as he wrote this letter. But then it occurred to him that they might be laboring under misinformation.

"Who could have told them these lies? What would give them the false impression that I have converted?" he asked himself. "It is incredible. My father wants me to send certification from a rabbi, but where in the world can I get hold of a rabbi? Perhaps I should write my father to send the rabbi from our town."

Merimzon wrote to his former melamed, Reuven, whose answer clarified how this misunderstanding had developed. Three months after Merimzon's own departure, chappers had caught another local boy and sent him to Kiev. The boy's father had followed the detachment surreptitiously. Finally, as they neared Kiev, he managed to steal his son back from the escort troops. This father had heard from someone near Kiev, and reported back to Merimzon's parents, that Merimzon's entire detachment had converted. Merimzon wrote to his parents that he had not betrayed his faith, and for all the remaining years of his service until his release to the reserves, Merimzon corresponded regularly with his parents.

The End of the Cantonist System

Soon after this incident, Tsar Alexander II ascended to the throne, and the government decided that the Cantonist army was useless to the state, wasting millions of rubles. The highly ranked officers of the Cantonist units competed with each other and received awards and promotions not for their military exploits, but for self-reports that they had converted the most Jews. A commander would circulate a report, "I have the honor to report that in the company entrusted to me, during such-and-such a period, such-and-such a number of Jews converted voluntarily."

Alexander now ordered that the Cantonist army be disbanded. The Russian soldiers who were below draft age were released immediately, but the Jewish Cantonists were handled differently. Converts to Christianity were transferred to various military training academies, to medical corpsman schools, and to training classes for clerks. Unconverted Jews were sent to the three Arakcheyev detachments in Petersburg, Moscow and Kiev. Soldiers in Merimzon's detachment were apprenticed out to work at a trade. Merimzon was sent to Moscow and apprenticed to a joiner.

Apprenticeship and Transformation

Merimzon was the only Jew in the joiners' shop among several masters and fifteen apprentices. They were of coarse peasant stock. Initially, they mocked and teased him, but he told himself, "Be not afraid, My servant Jacob!" and waited for better times.

Merimzon worked with diligence and gradually earned the respect of his co-workers. His boss started to give him gifts of money or cotton shirt cloth before holidays; the senior apprentices also gave him gifts. Merimzon was motivated to work even harder.

After a year, they seemed to accept him as one of their own. They gave him a Russian outfit: the boss's wife sewed him wide velveteen trousers and a side-fastening red shirt and the boss bought him a colorful silk sash with tassels and red-topped boots. The masters took Merimzon to the bathhouse and dressed him up in his Russian costume.

They stood him in the middle of the workshop and admired him. "Ah, he doesn't look like a Jew at all!" said the boss's wife. "Why don't you become Russian Orthodox like us? Honestly, you don't look like your people at all; they are so often dark, with hooked noses, but you look like a real Russian, one of us!"

"Yes, Natalya Petrovna," Merimzon said, understanding the need for diplomacy with his new friends. "I have been thinking about that for a long time myself, and I have learned all your prayers by heart, but I need to delay baptism until I finish my apprenticeship."

"May the Lord let it be so," she replied.

The young cook, Marfa, came running to take a look at the new Merimzon. He looked at her more closely too. Subsequently, despite the mutual attraction, he tried to avoid meeting her, but she did just the opposite.

On one occasion, the landlord, who liked Merimzon, gave him a ticket to the circus. When Marfa heard that he was going out, she asked for some time off to visit a girlfriend and contrived to meet him as if by chance.

She declared her love. "I have wanted to tell you for a long time that I have fallen madly in love with you. I want to marry you, but first you must convert. My dowry is two hundred rubles and a hut and garden in the village, and I will inherit nineteen acres of land. I will transfer all this to your name, but only to the name the priest gives you when you convert."

"Here's the thing, my dear Marfusha!" Merimzon hedged. "I have no objection to converting, but not yet — when I finish my apprenticeship. Then I shall convert, and we can be married. You'll be a cook, and I'll be a joiner; we'll earn a lot of money and open a shop like my master's. Then we will settle down and live wonderfully well. But for now, just wait a little while. I will love you until then."

"Ach, it's a long time to wait!" Marfa sighed.

Merimzon's boss had an elderly friend, a rich merchant and property owner named Vetrov. He personally sponsored a church and supported its clergy. The boss invited this wealthy man and his priest to celebrate his birthday.

At the table, the conversation turned to inheritances. Such-and-such a man had died and made a will, but such-and-such had not left a will, and now his heirs had taken the matter of how to divide his estate to court.

"I've already made a will," said Vetrov, who had lost his entire family to an epidemic. "I divided my estate into four parts: one part for monasteries, one for religious institutions, and one for the poor, widows and orphans. The fourth part is to go to a good, honest Jew, if I can find one and convert him to Christianity."

"I am having trouble finding such a person," he continued. "I have heard about people who get themselves converted, only to take the inheritance and go off to America! There they go back to being Jews again! In my opinion, that is blasphemy, and we, as Russian Orthodox people, should not stand for it."

"What do you think, Father? Am I being fair?" he asked the priest.

"Yes, you're quite right, but they're not all like that," said the priest. "I have had the opportunity to convert a few, and they turned out well and practiced our religion just like natural-born Russians. Just take your time in finding one."

"Just a moment, Maxim Kharitonovich," said Merimzon's boss. "Perhaps my Jewish apprentice could be persuaded to convert."

"Where did you get a Jew for an apprentice?" everyone asked.

"From the Arakcheyev detachment. I like this Jew better than any of my Russian apprentices. He has been with me for over two years, and I can say only good things about him. He's honest, conscientious, capable — in short, good in every way. If only he could be persuaded to convert! I have tried to talk him into it, but he always brushes me off. Maybe the Father can persuade him."

"Call him," said the priest.

Merimzon's boss called him from the workshop. As Merimzon dressed in his new clothes, he thought to himself, "I'm an ignoramus; how will I talk to a priest, an educated man from the academic world?" He entered, bowed low and stood near the door until he was invited to have a seat. They served him according to Russian custom — first vodka, then tea.

"Take a glass of vodka or wine and congratulate your boss on his name day," the priest said to Merimzon.

Knowing that Jews are not supposed to drink wine prepared by non-Jews, Merizon answered, "Father, I can congratulate him as well without wine, because I am not accustomed to liquor, and an apprentice is not supposed to drink wine."

Merimzon answered all the priest's questions about his origins, where he had served as a Cantonist soldier, his age, and how he had come to be in Moscow.

"I see that fate has brought you to Moscow for the sake of your good fortune. And you can have good fortune even now, if only you yourself do not refuse it."

"Father," said Merimzon, "who doesn't want to be kind to himself? Explain to me and teach me how to get good luck."

"Have you studied the Old Testament law of God?"

"I have," said Merimzon.

"Then you know that it says there that your people were chosen by God, but then God became angry with them and scattered them all over the world. Every nation has its own country, but your people have no refuge anywhere. I advise you to renounce your people and accept our Russian Orthodox faith and practice it conscientiously. Then you will be happy in this world and you will be allowed to enter the kingdom of heaven in the next world, because he who does not believe in Christ cannot go to the kingdom of heaven. There is where your good fortune lies. Take it!"

"Father," said Merimzon, "God's righteous judgment caused Him to become angry with my people and scatter them all over the world. Since He is Lord of the whole world, He scattered His chosen people over the whole world. You promise me riches in this world — but that, too, depends on God. You, Father, must have studied our ancient Hebrew language at the ecclesiastical academy. God says, *Li hakesef v'li hazahav* [Thy silver and thy gold are Mine: Hagai 2:8]."

"I must say to you that you hold your faith cheap, pressing it on every Jew like a shopkeeper hawking his wares. You are supposed to preach, 'Love thy neighbor.' That is how my boss, Ivan Vasilyevich, acts with me, though I am not a Christian, and why this esteemed merchant, Vetrov, is bequeathing his capital for worthy causes."

"Bravo! Bravo!" the guests cried, but the drunken priest turned red in the face and his eyes were bloodshot from malice and too much vodka.

Merimzon thought, "Now he's going to jump me and 'bless' me with his fists."

But the Father cleared his throat and stood up to leave.

"Sit a while longer, Father," said the host.

"No, I have to visit a dying man to administer the sacrament."

Everyone stood to receive his blessing, but he turned away from Merimzon and left.

"Well, you're a fine fellow, little Jew; you've exasperated our Priest. Well done!" said the boss.

The banquet ended and the guests started to leave. Vetrov pulled a purse as plump as a cushion out of his pocket and handed a three-ruble note to Merimzon. He patted him affectionately on the shoulder and said, "Well done, little Jew. Hold on to your faith."

"Thank you, sir!" said Merimzon.

From that time on, no one tried to pressure him to convert.

Near the end of the fourth year of Merimzon's apprenticeship, the boss died of a terminal disease. His wife sold their property and moved away with Marfa. The masters and apprentices went their separate ways. Merimzon left for command headquarters. He read the Twentieth Psalm of David, then approached a senior clerk to "grease his palm." The clerk agreed to replace Merimzon in the battalion with another soldier and transferred him to the Seventeenth division of the infantry, which was stationed in Saratov.

He waited at headquarters until they assembled a group for the trip, which passed through Nizhniy-Novogorod down the Volga to Saratov.

When the party arrived in Nizhniy, they had to wait again, and Merimzon became friendly there with a fellow Cantonist. The day before they were to depart, the two went to the market to buy food for the next leg of the journey.

Passover with the Subbotniks

It was the day before Passover. The two Jews walked and grieved; tomorrow their parents would sit at the Seder, while they would have to eat *chometz* (leavened food, forbidden during Passover) on the Volga. They reminisced about their lost childhoods and wept.

Suddenly, an elderly Russian approached. He was the paradigm of a genuine Russian merchant. He wore a long coat of dark blue broadcloth, belted with a red sash, his hair was cut square, and he had a broad, thick reddish beard.

He stopped the men and questioned them. From whence had they arrived? Where were they being sent? He did not ask their nationality, since he saw that they were Jews. He only asked whether they had been converted. Merimzon and his companion responded that they had not.

"I find that hard to believe," said the merchant. "You were in the Cantonists and were able to remain Jews? So where are you going now?"

They explained that they were on their way to buy bread.

"And tomorrow evening is the start of Passover!" said the merchant.

"What can we do, Herr Merchant? We aren't at liberty. It's the service!"

"Go back," he replied. "Don't spend your half-kopecks. I'll send you food for the whole trip, and within an hour, bring it to you myself." He hailed a cab and left.

Merimzon and his companion stood there in bewilderment. What did it mean? What did that merchant intend to do with them? Maybe he was insane or playing a joke. He didn't seem crazy, but who could be sure?

"We'll see," Merimzon said to his comrade. They went back to the assembly point to wait.

"Probably, as we were reminiscing and crying before, God accepted our tears and sent us *Eliyahu HaNavi* (Elijah the Prophet) disguised as a merchant," Merizon mused to his comrade. "We shall see. If he brings us food for Passover, we will know it is he."

They waited one hour, then another. Suddenly, the non-commissioned officer on duty came running with a note in his hand and shouted, "Which of you is Meyer Merimzon?"

Merimzon answered, "Here."

"Mikhail Zaks?"

"Here!" his comrade answered.

"The commander wants to see you," said the officer.

The pair went outside where a cabby waited. They were passing him on their way to the military commander, when he shouted out, "Hey, country boys! Aren't you Meyer Merimzon and Mikhail Zaks? I've come for you. Get in!"

They climbed into the cab. The cabby yanked on the reins, and the horse took off.

As they drove, Merimzon studied the cabby and he became suspicious. His clothes and appearance were more like a merchant's than a cabby. Merimzon whispered his suspicions to his comrade.

"What business is it of yours to figure out who he is? Just so he takes us where he's supposed to," Zaks whispered back.

They drove a few blocks and the driver stopped in a lane by a three-story house. He told them to get out and enter the wooden gate. In the yard, to their great surprise, they met the merchant who had promised to send them food. The "cabby" turned out to be his son.

The merchant led Merimzon and Zaks up a dark stairway to the very top floor. He opened the door of a large and lavishly appointed chamber. From the ceiling hung a bronze chandelier and pictures and mirrors in gilt frames hung on the walls. Velvet armchairs stood around the room.

At the large table with its colorful tablecloth, a middle-aged Jew in a long frock coat was reciting from the *Hagaddah* (the book used during the Passover meal). Two little boys with Russian features sat at his side. The Jew got up and offered the Cantonists his hand.

"Shalom aleichem," he said.

"Aleichem shalom," replied the boys.

Merimzon quietly asked the Jew, "Would you be so kind as to tell me what we have gotten into? What kind of people are these, half Russian, half Jew?"

The Jew smiled. "They are converts to Judaism. There are a fair number of converts here from the Subbotnik sect who enthusiastically practice our faith. The government persecutes them cruelly, but they have found a convenient place in my landlord's house, and they perform their religious rites here. I perform three jobs for them — *shochet* (butcher, ritual slaughterer), cantor and teacher. This evening they will gather here to sell their chometz, and tomorrow evening they will gather to pray."

The next night, the room was brightly lit by chandeliers and candles burning in silver candelabras. The table was laid lavishly, with a magnificent bottle of wine, small goblets at each place and a large goblet set aside for Elijah the prophet. At each end of the table was a china plate with three matzos, wrapped in new silk napkins. Pieces of horseradish and onions, boiled eggs and a dark brown mixture in little dishes were arranged decoratively on top of the napkins. The "kings" of the evening, the butcher and the host Avraham, sat at their places in armchairs covered with cushions with their "queens" at their sides.

The glasses were filled with wine, and the butcher placed his glass upon his right palm and recited the Kiddush in the traditional melody. Then he invited the soldiers to recite the Kiddush. Merimzon remembered how he used to do it at home and he chanted the words with joy, clearly and distinctly. His comrade, Mikhail, followed suit. Two little boys who had memorized the Four Questions rattled them off fluently, and all joined together to answer the questions.

Soon, *knaidlach* (matzah balls) were served with tasty soup and a large portion of goose. After the food, the seder continued, and everyone sang merrily with the help of the several cups of wine each had downed. When the cantor signaled to open the front door for Elijah the Prophet, everyone cried out, *Baruch habo* (welcome)! The final song of *Chad Gadya* (One Little Goat) was sung to the lively tune of a Russian *kamarinskaya* (folk dance). The seder lasted until long after midnight.

Exhausted, Merimzon and his friend slept in soft beds until the morning, when the butcher called them, "Morning prayers!" It was quite a change from the wake-up calls they had heard over the past several years.

After the morning prayers, everyone else left, but they were bid to remain longer, through the holiday week. They did not need much urging and found themselves back in the dining room, offering toasts. "L'Chaim!"

On the first day of *Chol HaMoed* (intermediate days of the holiday week), when the community gathered for tea, a conversation started over the two guests. The host told how he had met them and had managed to persuade the army commander to grant them temporary leave.

"Ach, Avraham Moisevich, you have done them a great service. And you have earned salvation for your soul from our true God. After all, had it not been for you, the poor boys would have had to eat chometz."

"I would like to earn that kind of credit with God," said another. "We should help them. An open hand is never empty. We'll pool our resources. If anyone wants to make a donation, bring it after havdala."

"Very well," they all agreed.

And so, Merimzon and Zaks spent Passover in comfort they had never imagined. They were content, well fed, and at peace.

When the final day of the holiday arrived, the Cantonists were due to take leave of paradise and return to hell. Avraham Moisevich was still chanting havdala when members of the community, men and women, arrived bearing gifts. They brought cotton for shirts, ticking for underclothes, towels, linen for foot cloths, handkerchiefs — in short, a whole bagful of gifts, not to mention food. The wife of the butcher gave them a little prayer book.

The butcher put a plate on the table and started a collection by throwing in a silver coin. Coins of all values poured in after it until the whole plate was full. The children, seeing the adults donating money to the Cantonists, begged their parents for the honor of contributing some kopecks for their guests. The parents cheerfully gave them each a coin, and the children threw the money into the plate and went away with their little faces shining.

The host gave the Cantonists a ruble each. "Listen, boys, hold on to our holy faith. Don't be tempted when someone promises you riches or rank. Don't put your trust in idols, and go on believing in the God of Abraham, Isaac and Jacob. Stand firm!"

"Thank you, grandfather, for your exhortation," they replied.

Merimzon's heart ached in anguish at the thought that tomorrow he would have to part from these good people. He remembered the melancholy hymn, *Adir Nora V'Ayom, B'Saar Lecha Ekra* (Mighty One, Awesome One, and Devastating One, when I am in trouble, I call to You),[125] and he sang it loudly through his tears. The butcher tried to comfort Merimzon, but Merimzon couldn't control his sobs.

Everyone watching him weep asked the butcher, "What kind of song is that, that he bursts into tears that way?" The butcher translated it into Russian; they sighed deeply and also tried to comfort Merimzon. The guests bid goodbye to the Cantonists and went on their way.

Back to the Army

In the morning, their benefactor, Avraham Moisevich and his wife delivered them back to their commander, just as parents see off their beloved sons on a long journey. They were escorted right to the dock and bid farewell to their benefactor, his wife and son as though they were their family. They boarded a wooden barge that was hitched to a steamboat. The steamboat started off down the river. They knew they were back in the army world when a group of drunken soldiers started to sing, "Down Mother Volga, on its broad expanse;" the Cantonists recited the traditional Jewish travelers' prayer.

In Saratov, they reported to the headquarters of the Seventeenth Infantry Division. A young officer ran out of the receiving hall, calling, "Which of you is Merimzon?"

Merimzon stood at attention and said, "Here, your honor!"

"Where were you sent here from?"

"From the Arakcheyev detachment in Moscow, your honor!"

"And where were you with the Cantonists?"

"In the Kiev battalion, your honor."

"And did you know a Grinblat?"

"Yes, your honor; he was inducted with me."

The officer had more questions and wanted to continue the inquiry, but the duty officer interrupted him, "Sir, the division commander is looking for you."

The officer hurried into his coat and left. Merimzon knew at once that the officer was referring to his friend Klezmer, renamed Grinblat by the induction officer, whom the chappers had turned in with him when they were children. But how had the officer known to ask him about this friend? Merimzon wanted to find out more but didn't know whom to ask.

They divided the Cantonists up by regiments, and Merimzon and Zaks were separated. Merimzon went to the Sixty-sixth Infantry Butyrskiy regiment.

Eventually, he invited a senior clerk who could tell him about the young officer to a tavern and entertained him in the Russian manner. The clerk told him that the officer had come to the regiment from a Junker academy with a first-class rating and had served as regimental adjutant and as company commander. He had distinguished himself in corps review. For his outstanding service he had been promoted and transferred to Tashkent. And the officer was a convert to Christianity. When Merimzon heard this, he heaved a sigh. Grinblat had buckled under the pressure.

Merimzon was assigned to a formation when he joined his army regiment in 1862. He was adept with a rifle and earned praise from the company commander for his skill. Soon Merimzon was recommended for non-commissioned officer training.[126] Merimzon was thrilled with his improved prospects, but fate was preparing an even more pleasant surprise for him.

Medical Training

At the start of the Polish uprising in 1862, the Military Medical Command Headquarters decided that the armed forces needed more medical corpsmen. A circular announced the establishment of a corpsman school at each regiment's infirmary. Sixteen able young soldiers, one man from each company, would be selected for training.

Merimzon's division doctor was sympathetic towards the Jews, and he directed the senior regimental physicians to admit a few more of the "little Jews." The soldiers lined up for a regimental review, and the senior regimental physician strode down the line, calling out, "Jews, step forward!"

The Jews who stepped out were all older soldiers and would soon be retiring. The doctor approached Merimzon's company and shouted out, "Jews, step forward!" Five men stepped forward, of whom Merimzon was the youngest. The doctor didn't ask him any questions, simply instructed that his name be taken down. Merimzon turned in his rifle and reported to the regimental infirmary.

As Merimzon walked to the infirmary, he thought, "Can you beat that? I thought I was joining a training detachment, but I've gotten into medical school. What a contrast there is between those institutions!"

Merimzon arrived at the infirmary where fifteen men had already gathered. They were to be taught an abbreviated version of everything a corpsman needed to know, with an emphasis on bandaging.

Merimzon was the only Jew in the group, and he alone could neither read nor write Russian. The others were Poles, Latvians and Russians, who could read and write Russian quite well. The Poles could also read some Latin. Merimzon realized he would need to study independently to catch up with the others. He bought a Russian and a Latin alphabet book and applied himself with great diligence. Within a month, Merimzon had learned to read Russian fluently and could manage with Latin as well. After three months he had caught up.

He soon began treating patients with attention and consideration. He copied out the Lunin corpsman's textbook for himself and carefully observed the work of the experienced medical corpsmen. Merimzon was always studying his textbook, and by the end of the first year, the corpsmen had started asking Merimzon to tend their patients. The senior physician started to pay special attention to Merimzon.

During the second year of studies, the conflict with Poland came to a boil, and mobilization began. The Tsar's government thought that France would come in on the side of the Poles. Merimzon's division was assigned to suppress the uprising in Poland. The route was laid out along the Volga towards the Polish border by way of Nizhniy-Novogorod. They steamed to Nizhniy but received a telegram commanding their division to stop there, because there were already enough troops in place.

Merimzon lived comfortably for two years as a junior corpsman until 1868. He continued to care for his patients, checking their temperatures or dispensing medicine. He was paid for his work and saved some money. He became popular among the workers who came to him for advice. He was accepted among his peers and was invited to weddings, name days and christenings. He was a favorite everywhere, despite the fact that he was a Jew.

New military regulations enacted in 1874 reduced the term of service for those inducted under the old recruitment regulations. All the years spent in the armed forces would be taken into account for former Cantonist soldiers, whereas previously, only service after the age of twenty had been counted. The end of his military service was drawing near, and it was only a matter of time before Merimzon would be on his way back home.

Merimzon decided to brush up his knowledge of Hebrew and Judaism so as not to return home an ignoramus. He befriended a kosher butcher and took lessons from him. At first, his teacher reviewed the material that Merimzon had studied long ago in cheder, then he translated for him from Hebrew into Russian. Merimzon's renewed Jewish studies were soon interrupted when his division was transferred to a camp near Moscow. His teacher gave Merimzon a little book with vernacular translation and he used it to cram diligently.

From the camp, Merimzon's division was transferred to Tula, where he served until he was transferred to the reserves.

Going Home, Twenty Years Later

At the end of his service, Merimzon considered staying in Tula and working at a hospital or the *zemstvo* (district council). However, he felt drawn to his family, his home country, and his own people. And so, Merimzon headed back to the Jewish Pale of Settlement.

Before he reached his hometown, he stopped in Kovno and bought tzitzit and tefillin from the local scribe. The scribe taught Merimzon how to put on the tefillin and what prayers to recite. His wife sewed the tzitzit onto his garment.

Merimzon set out by train for his hometown in high spirits. After all his years of suffering, he was finally going home to his beloved parents. This was the final leg of the ill-fated trip to the tavern twenty years earlier.

He arrived in his town before dawn and saw a light burning in one house. He looked through the window and saw a baker putting rolls into an oven, and an elderly woman sitting on a bed and rocking slightly as she read Psalms. He went into the bakery and asked about his parents.

The couple assumed from his uniform that he was a policeman and were petrified with fear.

The baker hurriedly set out a stool. "Sit down, sir!"

Merimzon calmed them, "I am a Jew; I was born here."

The old woman closed her prayer book, and the baker put his paddle in the corner. They asked him to whom he belonged, and Merimzon told them.

The old women cried out, "Ach, it's you, Chaimka!" She told her husband, "Nachum, quickly, do a mitzva, go tell his parents!" Merimzon suggested that they go together.

As they went into his parents' hut, Merimzon was struck by its wretched appearance and by their poverty. His heart sank and tears filled his eyes. Meanwhile, the old woman and Nachum were congratulating Merimzon's parents on their unexpected guest. Merimzon's parents looked at him wildly and shouted angrily at the bakers, "Why do you laugh at us? Shame on you for mocking us! You amuse yourselves with our misfortune! Don't open up wounds that have almost healed! We have begun to forget about him."

"Reb Yosef! Merele! Why are you angry?" Nachum and his wife insisted. "This is your son, for goodness sake."

"No, our former son abandoned our holy faith long ago. We have kept it a secret until now out of shame."

"And why does he know your name, if it isn't he?"

"Maybe this *orl* [imposter] served with our son and got the address from him. Oh, Reb Nachum, please tell him to go to his own parents. You know how to talk to him, let him not harass us. Be so kind, please, tell this sergeant to leave!" With these words, Merimzon's father turned and left for the beit midrash for the morning service.

Nachum and his wife tried to reason with Merimzon's mother. "Look, this soldier is a Jew and he speaks Yiddish."

"And do no gentiles speak Yiddish?" his mother countered. "How can you assure me that he is our son, when you yourselves have just seen him now for the first time? Take him and go away, for God's sake!"

Merimzon stood like a statue throughout this exchange. He longed to throw himself on his mother's neck and rejoice that she was still alive, but he realized that this would frighten her to death.

Merimzon went to the inn, where he reflected on how, not long ago, he had been making plans for a joyful family reunion. His family hadn't even recognized him. His bitter thoughts were interrupted by a synagogue sexton who summoned Merimzon to the rabbi. Merimzon knew he would be questioned to ascertain the validity of his claims, and took along his Jewish prayer items as material evidence.

The rabbi observed the coat of Merimzon's dress uniform and shrugged his shoulders. "How, my son, can you prove that you haven't converted?" he asked.

"Here is the first proof for you." Merimzon unfastened his coat and showed him that he was wearing not a cross, but tzitzit. "And here is the second," and he showed him the pouch containing his tefillin, "And the third," his siddur.

Seeking incontrovertible evidence, the rabbi asked to see Merimzon's reserve card. He sent for a clerk from the local troops who spoke Russian and who happened to be a Jew. The clerk verified that Merimzon's army identity papers listed him as a Jew. The rabbi was finally convinced and blessed Merimzon, laying his hands on his head.

The sexton promptly fetched Merimzon's parents. The rabbi greeted them merrily and announced, "Now you can be sure than your son is a Jew. He can even be called 'a righteous one' because he has endured such suffering for our faith. May God give me even a small part of his reward in the afterlife!"

When they heard these words, Merimzon's parents were transformed in the blink of an eye. His mother flung her arms around his neck. She pressed his head to her breast and wailed, "My dear, darling little boy! My darling kaddish! Forgive us for mistreating you, for repaying your good with evil! May our enemies hang themselves! Please forgive us!"

"My dear parents," said Merimzon, "it is you who must forgive me. I was never angry with you. I knew that someone lied to you and told you that I had betrayed our holy faith. Perhaps because of your prayers, I have survived. Perhaps because your tears reached up to God, I have been granted the privilege of seeing you again."

Merimzon's father embraced his wife and son, and they all cried tears of joy.

The rabbi's wife, hearing the laughter and tears, asked, "Why are you crying? Be happy and thank God that he has come home at last. Now lead him *l'Torah ul'chupah ul'maasim tovim* (to a life of Torah observance and study, marriage, and good deeds)."

"Amen!" said the rabbi.

Merimzon and his parents got up and went back to their hut. A happy bustling began. His mother ran to get herring and his father went for vodka. The table was ready in a few minutes. He poured a glass, and declared, "I am happy, my dear parents, that thanks to your prayers, God has protected me to see you again. L'chaim!"

"We, too, are glad," his father answered, "that God has extended our lifetime and considered us worthy to see you. It is to your credit that you sacrificed yourself and bore the yoke in the name of our holy faith. L'chaim, my son! May God let us lead you to the chupah with a good *ziveg* (match). Amen!"

An Upstanding Member of the Community

When the townspeople found out that Merimzon was a doctor, one matchmaker arrived after another. Each lavished praise upon a particular bride. Merimzon's mother, however, familiar with all the prospective brides, refused all the middlemen and looked for a bride herself. She took him to a bride show and introduced him to a rosy-cheeked woman, older then most of the prospective brides, who appeared healthy and well-fed. Merimzon looked into her eyes, observed her manners, and concluded that she was none too clever, but his mother assured him that she was "neither a candle for God nor a poker for the devil."

Both sets of parents were in a hurry to formalize the engagement so that the wedding could be held quickly, but Merimzon had serious reservations.

"Please don't rush things. Let me look around and get to know the local conditions and languages (Lithuanian, Polish and German). I'm not even sure yet about my doctor's practice. Just wait a while," he beseeched them.

"Oh, my son, we have waited long enough. One day is a lifetime to us. Why put it off?" Merimzon's mother objected.

They started bringing the dressed-up bride to the house, but the moment Merimzon saw her he would leave.

His mother realized that he didn't like his fianceè and she reproached him, "Why are you acting like such a big shot, my son? Her parents are giving you the girl with a dowry of three hundred rubles, and you're throwing your weight around. You're nothing but a soldier! Is the daughter of a respectable family given to a soldier? It's only because our family is of prominent descent. No, you must become fond of the girl, son, we like her."

The commandment to honor one's parents seemed to Merimzon enough reason to overcome his objections, and he agreed to the engagement party. They broke pots and jugs as was the custom, crying out, "Mazel Tov, Mazel Tov!" The bride's father handed over the dowry. The two sets of parents called on each other every day for tea, and they sent the young couple to get to know one another on walks around town.

On one of these walks with his bride-to-be, Merimzon asked her about her father's affairs, hoping to get a better idea of her intelligence. In response to his questions, she burst into wild laughter that sounded like a gun firing.

"Why are you laughing?" asked Merimzon.

"I was just remembering how the cat caught a mouse today and when my mother was chasing it out, she almost fell over the threshold!" His bride laughed some more.

"Well," Merimzon thought, "I'm done for. An agreement has been signed before three witnesses, the dishes have been broken, the dowry has been delivered, and — the main thing — my mother likes her. What in the world can I do? After all, not everyone can have a smart woman for a wife, and where are the fools to go?"

When Merimzon returned home he found the tailor, come to take measurements for the wedding coat. He asked him to make it as short as possible, but even on this point he was overruled. His mother insisted that it reach down to his very heels.

"According to our law, my dear son, you can't stand under the wedding canopy in a short coat. People will laugh at you and call you a German Jew!"

The next day the tailor brought the coat, Merimzon's father's belt was tied about his waist, his shoes were blackened with pitch, and a *yarmulka* (skullcap) was placed on his head topped by his father's holiday shtreimel. Merimzon was led to the wedding canopy.

His mother whispered to his father, "Look, old man, how our son is shining like a bright sun, as though the holy spirit were soaring above him; it's just a shame that his side locks haven't had time to grow out." The bride was hidden under a veil.

Merimzon reluctantly said the words, "Behold you are consecrated unto me by the laws of Moses and Israel." He angrily crushed the wineglass under his heel.

The young couple sat, like a tsar and tsarina, or rather like a gander and a turkey hen. They ate their golden soup with chicken. The men feasted, the young people danced. Merimzon's mother danced the "kosher dance" with his mother-in-law, and with that the wedding ended. Merimzon was a married man.

Merimzon set up his medical practice and furnished himself with the appropriate medicines. Local Jews began coming for medical care, mostly for gastric disorders. The fee, fifteen kopecks per visit, had been established long ago by the Kahal. Merimzon loaded his pockets with copper coins, but when he counted his first week's pay, it turned out that he had only earned enough to buy salt, pepper, and onions. For the rest he had to dip into the dowry money.

The following week, Lithuanian non-Jews started coming on the recommendation of the Jewish patients, but Merimzon didn't know Lithuanian and had to hire an interpreter. Then Poles started to show up as well, and Merimzon had to add Polish to his repertoire. On market day his patients would gather and when they all started to talk, each in his own language, a Tower of Babel would form in his brain from the confusion.

Merimzon's aged parents died soon after his return from the service. After three years of medical practice, Merimzon finally gave up on the Babel of languages in the Pale of Settlement and returned to Russia. He found a job with the zemstvo of the Bryansk District, Orlovsky Province, which turned out well. Later, he worked at the city hospital in Bryansk, and after that he had his own practice.

The years passed. His family life fell into place. But toward the end of his life he felt lonely and abandoned.

Eliyakum Zunser:
A Songwriter's Tale

Eliyakum Zunser was a renowned writer, poet, lyricist and composer whose work was popular among Russian Jews. In this adapted excerpt from his autobiography, he recalls the circumstances in which several of his best-loved works were composed.[127]

Eliyakum Zunser was sent to work in the city of Boisk before even reaching his *bar mitzvah* (age thirteen, when Jewish boys are considered responsible for their actions and deeds). One day, he received a letter from his mother with the news that his nine-year-old brother, Akiva, had been drafted. Zunser was distraught and walked the long distance home from Boisk to Vilna to be with his mother.

Zunser's weeping mother embraced him when he arrived.

"Now you are my only one! I have no one else in the world!" she sobbed. "It happened at night. Akiva and I were reciting the *Shema* [prayer "Hear O Israel"] before he went to bed. Suddenly, the chappers burst in. I struggled like a tigress, but they overpowered me. The child was torn away from me and carried off. They knocked me to the floor and beat me where I lay. The thick, heavy army coat was placed upon Akiva and he was sent off to Siberia."

The law explicitly stated that only families with three or more children were required to send a son to the army. Legally, Zunser's family was exempt from service because the widowed mother had only two children. But this law was rarely enforced and was ignored by the chappers.

Zunser had little opportunity to mourn his brother's fate. His mother could not support him, and he had to work for his living. Zunser was a good embroiderer, but he could not work locally because he was bound by a six-year contract to his former master if he remained in the vicinity. He bid goodbye to his mother and started off on foot into the world.

Zunser arrived in the city of Bobruisk in the district of Minsk on the first day of the Hebrew month of Elul in the Jewish year 5613, which was 1853 by the secular calendar. For several days he wandered the streets of Bobruisk but could find no embroiderer with whom to work.

Zunser had musical talent and thought he might earn his living as a vocalist. He approached the renowned *chazzan* (cantor) Reb Joel I. Houminer who chanted *musaf* (additional prayers on Sabbath and holidays) during the High Holy Days. Houminer heard Zunser sing and found that he possessed a good voice and a fine ear. He engaged Zunser to sing for the holidays at the salary of two rubles and secured him board at the home of the synagogue president.

Zunser composed two songs for the occasion: "The Light" and "Reb Tahanun." The latter was an instant hit and was sung everywhere.

During the holiday of Sukkot, Zunser spent the evening of *Simchat Beit Hashoevah*[128] in the house of the president of the synagogue. The choir sang his song, "Reb Tahanun," and the Hasidim were delighted with the young songwriter.

But when the holidays were over, Houminer paid Zunser his two rubles and told him his work was finished. Zunser had to leave.

It was autumn, and the weather was turning cold. Zunser had only his thin summer clothes. He bought a coat in the market with the two rubles he had earned, but he was still concerned about how he would survive the freezing winter.

A few days later, roaming the streets of Bobruisk, Zunser met a farmer who lived outside the city and was seeking a Hebrew tutor for his children. Zunser offered his services. The salary was twenty-five rubles for the term of six months, with the additional privilege of sleeping on the farmer's warm oven.

Zunser taught his students six hours a day. Since his clothes were wearing out and were not warm enough for the winter, he asked the farmer for an advance on his salary with which to purchase warmer garments. His employer put him off, saying that he should stay for a second term, and then he would pay him in full after the end of the entire period.

Zunser felt that he was in no position to argue.

At the time of the Shavuot holiday in the late spring, the farmer again made excuses to Zunser for not paying him. This time, Zunser demanded his rightful payment.

The farmer approached the leaders of the Kahal in Bobruisk. For a price, he offered them a Cantonist recruit. He was paid twenty-five rubles and returned home with a chapper and two Cossacks. Zunser was sleeping when the three strangers woke him. One held a lantern close to his eyes and stunned him with a blow to the face. He was wrapped in his worn clothes, bound like a sheep, thrown into a wagon, and taken to Bobruisk, where he was locked up in the barracks.

Zunser was held with other recruits for weeks. The authorities were not scrupulous regarding whom they seized, and the weak, sick and defective were all being held for service. These unfortunates took the places of boys whose families could pay a bribe for their freedom. The Kahal deputies divided the ransom money among themselves.

Many private individuals engaged in this traffic, seizing young children and selling them to the Kahal "bosses." Reminiscent of the sale of Joseph by his own brothers, these betrayals occurred daily. Lesser rabbis of small towns assented to such transactions, rationalizing that it was more "pious" to save the children of their own towns than to concern themselves with the fate of strangers.

Though many important rabbis wept at these outrages, most dared not protest. They were afraid of the consequences if the Jewish community would defy the Tsar's quota. The rabbis held their positions at the discretion of the Kahal leaders and feared the consequences of displeasing them. They were afraid to be denounced to government officials and exiled to Siberia.

Now fourteen, Zunser anticipated a long, hard life as a Cantonist. Eighty miserable, pale, emaciated, hungry, half-naked little beings lay in a heap on the floor of the barracks on a pile of dirty straw. Most were small children who had been snatched from their mothers. The young ones did not realize the gravity of their situation but the older Cantonists shed bitter tears. Twice daily a Kahal employee opened the iron barracks doors and delivered some loaves of bread and a few pots of dirty soup. Anyone who complained was seized by the hair and thrust against the wall with enough force to crack his young bones.

When night arrived, all the boys lay in the dirty straw and recited the Shema. The older boys recited Psalms by heart and lulled themselves to sleep. Here and there a heavy sigh broke forth.

Zunser formed a ten-boy choir and taught them a song he had written called "The Captives." When the sad strains of the music echoed through the barracks, even their jailers wept.

But help was nearer than any of the boys could have known. Six months after Zunser had been seized, Tsar Nicholas I died suddenly. Alexander II ascended the Russian throne, the treaty of Paris was signed, and the Crimean War came to an end. One of the very first edicts issued by Alexander II was for the release of the captured recruits.

On the night of the twenty-sixth of August, the cancellation of the Cantonist Recruitment Decree became official. At one o'clock in the morning, the sleeping boys were awakened by a commotion from the street outside the barracks. The mob came nearer and soon they heard pounding on the iron doors and shutters.

"Get up, children! Deliverance! You are free!" someone shouted.

"An order from the Tsar to release you!" shouted another.

"Praise God, children! Say *Hallel!*"[130] several voices called out together.

With a cry of joy, the children sprang from their wretched straw and washed so they could recite Hallel. Zunser was the cantor and his choir accompanied him. The boys joined hands and danced. On the spot, Zunser composed and arranged the melodious song "*Die Yeshua* (The Deliverance)."

A crowd of men and women, young and old, gathered around the doors of the barracks waiting impatiently for the moment when the boys would emerge. All praised and blessed the good Tsar Alexander II.

Wealthy Reb Isaac Rabinovitz of Bobruisk donated forty rubles to the synagogue for the privilege of opening the door to the barracks at ten o'clock the next morning. With the benediction, "Blessed be He that releases them that are bound," Rabinovitz unlocked the door and the crowd surged into the barracks. The town chazzan recited a prayer for the Tsar and sang the Forty-fifth Psalm, "I waited patiently for the Lord; He inclined unto me and heard me cry."

Zunser and his choir were lifted onto a large table and they sang his song "Placed Before the Bar of Justice and Convicted." Many of the people wept. But the song also had another effect. The people became so enraged at the Kahal bosses, who had already gone into hiding, that they were ready to tear them to pieces.

Zunser sang two more of his own songs, "The Deliverance" and "Better to Take Than to Give," which described the chicanery of the farmer. This song evoked a storm of indignation and wrath from the crowd. Many were ready to go to the village and lynch the farmer on the spot, but Reb Isaac Rabinovitz himself promised to deal with the matter. The barracks door was thrown wide and the eighty children surged forth, singing. Reb Rabinovitz took Zunser home with him in his carriage.

With the help of his sponsor, Zunser acquired some wealth of his own. Reb Isaac Rabinovitz sent for the farmer and ordered him to pay Zunser his fifty rubles back pay plus the twenty-five rubles he had received for turning in Zunser to the Kahal. The farmer pleaded poverty, but Rabinovitz sent several Cossacks to his village to seize the contents of his house. A few days later, the farmer arrived with seventy-five rubles and redeemed his belongings.

Zunser was suddenly a wealthy man. In fact he felt himself to be practically a Rothschild. From time to time, Rabinovitz's guests also paid him to sing the three songs he had composed in the barracks.

One morning, when Zunser had been living at Rabinovitz's house for some time, the servant informed him that someone wished to see him. Zunser went to the door and was overjoyed to see his mother and uncle. Zunser's mother clasped him in her arms and wept. She explained that she had received a letter from an acquaintance with the news of Zunser's capture. She had obtained a passport for him from the Vilna Kahal and, accompanied by his uncle, walked the fifty versts (approximately thirty kilometers) to Bobruisk to free him. The reunited family spent eight days at Rabinovitz's house.

Zunser returned to his mother's home in Vilna. Seeing her poverty reminded him of the necessity to earn his own living. His contract with his first master-embroiderer still prevented him from working locally. So Zunser again left his mother in Vilna and ventured forth to seek his fortune in the world.

The Story of Bentse the Chapper

This story can be read as a morality tale. It describes the life of a man who served the Kahal as a chapper.
Adapted from S. Beylin, Memoirs From the Last Years of Recruitment, Yevreiskaya Starina, *Volume VII, 1914, 459–462.*

There was a chapper in the town of Novogrudok by the name of Bentse der Chapper, or Bentse *der mishores* (servant of the community). He was a heavyset man with a thick, bull neck and a hefty belly. The mothers in the town feared Bentse, who would kidnap their sons and turn them over to be soldiers. They heaped many curses upon Bentse's head. Indeed, many of those curses came true at the end of Bentse's life.

The Kahal administration paid good money to the chappers during the era of the Cantonists. Bentse would seize young people, primarily the poor and indigent, and turn them in for soldiers. The induction of recruits usually took place long before the Jewish New Year, but Bentse would seize boys right after tilling, in September or October, when they were not expecting danger.

The boys who had been seized were fed heartily on delicacies. They ate roast goose and *gribbenes* (crisp onions and chicken skin fried in chicken fat), white bread and buns. They were given copious quantities of vodka. The Kahal employees pampered the captives in an attempt to persuade them to "volunteer" for the army in return for two or three hundred rubles. A volunteer had to declare to the authorities that he was joining the army of his own free will, taking the place of someone else. The Jewish community was empowered to turn in a volunteer in place of a person due for induction, or to turn him in for a credit receipt which could be given later to a person wanting (and ready to pay for) an exemption.

Some of the detainees became violent and started brawls as they passed the time under guard, waiting for induction. Others played cards and drank heavily. The Kahal hirelings egged them on, feigning delight in their boldness and bravado. The Kahal bosses cited the debauched behavior as justification of their own actions.

"They say the fellow is hopeless anyway, depraved, a reveler, a real *okhotnik* [ne'er-do-well];[131] A decent, God-fearing young man, the son of a good *baleboss* [established member of the community] after all, would never be turned in..."

Many older captives who had no trade or source of income resigned themselves to their predicament and agreed to accept payment in exchange for volunteering. Things had been difficult for them when they were free, anyway. They had been idle, cold and hungry, for months at a time. At least now they were warm and well fed. And they knew that they could be turned in even if they did not go voluntarily. The Kahal had absolute power in the community to establish the order of induction.

But in most cases, the detainees were in despair. They cried, cursed, wrung their hands and tore their hair. They attempted escape at every opportunity, up to the moment of induction, scorning the inducements and the financial reward offered by the parents of the "next in line."

On a typical night, howling and crying awoke the villagers in Novogrudok. New captives were being taken to the police station. In the morning, they saw the prisoners through the iron bars of the window. Among them was Leibechke der Batlan, a vagabond at the public bathhouse, Lipechke der Shaygets, a street brawler, and Leibechke der Kishenik, a local pickpocket.

The captives sang mournful prayers, compositions of the town chazzan. Their melancholy melodies caused everyone who passed to sigh in pity for the unfortunate ones.

"They sing, poor wretches, to forget their terrible sorrow."

When Alexander II abolished the Recruitment Decree, the Kahal no longer required the services of chappers. Bentse the Chapper's salary was reduced gradually until it stopped altogether. He could not even find work as a laborer in poor Novogrudok.

With this decrease in Bentse's status, his son-in-law left his daughter. The son-in-law had married Bentse's daughter only to secure Bentse's protection from recruitment. The son-in-law reasoned that it would now be to his disadvantage to be connected to the family of a has-been servant of the Kahal.

Bentse's children went into service. His daughters became children's nurses and his son became a clerk.

By 1881, Bentse bore no resemblance to his former stout self. The hunched old man's face showed, as clearly as if it had been written there, that he often went hungry. In addition he was almost blind. His only earnings were the thirty or forty kopeck fees he occasionally received for calling the members of the community to some public meeting, or for calling guests to weddings, circumcisions, or betrothals, for which he received a couple of zlotys.

Once, a tender-hearted shopkeeper's wife caught sight of Bentse, hardly able to drag himself along, weak and sickly.

"Good heavens, he is a walking corpse!" she cried out with tears in her eyes. "He is wasting away from hunger. Lord, where is justice? Even horses are not abandoned when they get old. Bentse served the Kahal faithfully." She believed that Bentse, as a servant of the Kahal, was just a tool in the hands of the community. He had become a scapegoat for their sins.

Bentse, remarkably enough, blamed no one for his fate. He had become painfully isolated. Morning and evening, one saw him walk punctually to the synagogue. There he took a humble place near the door and prayed quietly, devoutly, his face contrite. On the Sabbath he would pull on his tattered Sabbath clothing and walk sedately from his apartment on the outskirts of town to the synagogue and back, gazing into the distance with dim eyes. He gave the impression that, exhausted by hunger, he might fall down in the street at any moment.

The old man accepted the blows of fate with humility. He bore the death of his only son and breadwinner without a murmur. His son, young and handsome, literate in Russian, had held the position of clerk to the district police officer and had been paid twenty-five rubles a month. The son had caught a chill and died of galloping consumption.

The death of his son was the last straw for Bentse. He died in 1883 of chronic hunger and cold.

Before he died, Bentse believed that his misfortunes were atonement for the sins he had committed during the years of the old recruitment system. Clearly a spark of God still glimmered in the soul of the former chapper. In essence, he atoned not only for his own personal sins, but for the sins of his entire generation.

Appendix of Documents

Inductee's Oath

The following oath was mandatory for every Cantonist who was inducted into the Russian army. The inductee read the oath aloud in Yiddish and Hebrew in front of witnesses from the Jewish community and the local government. The oath was translated into Russian and signed by a Jewish court and a quorum of ten witnesses.

From: Saul M. Ginsburg, Historishe Verk, Yiddishe Leiden in Tsarishen Russland, *(Historical Work, Jewish Martyrdom in Tsarist Russia), 1915, Volume III, page 9.*

I swear in the name of God, the God of the Jews, that I will serve the Russian Tsar and the Russian Empire. No matter what they ask of me during my stint of duty, I will fulfill it with humility and faithfulness. I will do everything to ensure the success of our land and our Holy Torah. I will never forsake this promise, either publicly or in my heart. I am sworn by those who made me swear, and everything that I may say after, or have said previously, shall be considered null and void. God forbid that I should seek a way out of this oath. However, if I do sin and transgress this oath and do not work diligently as a faithful servant, my family and I will be excommunicated, both in this world and the world to come.

Imperial Command for Baptism

This letter contains the 1830 order instructing army personnel to "allow" Jewish recruits to accept Christianity and to provide religious instruction in the "chosen" denomination.

> From: I. Galant, Documents From the Era of Nicholas I, Yevreiskaya Starina, *Volume VII, 1914, p.104.*

Ministry of Internal Affairs, Executive Police Department.

Division 2, Desk 2.

September 6, 1830, No. 2591.

Mr. Civil Governor:

His Imperial Majesty has been pleased to issue an Imperial Command: that Jews inducted as recruits shall be permitted to accept the Christian faith of all creeds tolerated in Russia. That they shall be dispatched according to assignment, however, without being held at the recruitment location, in compliance with the regulations promulgated on the latter subject. The commanders of the troops to which they are assigned, having received appropriate notification of their professed wish, are to see to their instruction in the tolerated Christian denomination of their choice and their affiliation with it, according to law, by the spiritual leaders of the designated denominations. I hasten to inform Your Excellency of this command by His Imperial Majesty for the purpose of its appropriate execution, hereby commissioning you to notify me without delay concerning your arrangements.

Signed,

Minister of Internal Affairs

Adjutant-General Zakrevskiy

Penalties for the Family and Community of a Self-Mutilator

In 1837, the State Council, after reviewing the presentation of the Ministry of Internal Affairs on the subject of potential recruits who intentionally mutilated themselves, introduced the following article into the recruiting regulations.

From: H. Khorobkov, "Recruitment of Jews During the Reign of Nicholas I," Yevreiskaya Starina, Volume VI, 1913, p. 234.

If anyone in a Jewish family whose turn has come up does injury to himself in order to avoid military service, he is to be taken as a recruit in any event, despite the injury. In addition, from his family, both in substitution for the person who has rendered himself unfit for service and in punishment for his family having failed to restrain him from the mutilation, another able-bodied recruit, preferably an underage recruit, will be taken by order of the authorities. These two recruits are to be counted as one for that family. Moreover, the community to which the family of the mutilator belongs is credited with an additional one-third of a recruit for the mutilator, over and above the able-bodied recruit taken for service.

Penalties for Jews who Incite Draft Evasion

This opinion of the State Council of November 27, 1838, approved by the Tsar, defines the penalties for inciting servicemen to evade military service.

From: H. Khorobkov, H. Recruitment of Jews During the Reign of Nicholas I, Yevreiskaya Starina, *Volume VI, 1913, p. 239.*

Jews who incite their fellow Jews to escape from military service or who help them hide shall be turned in as recruits themselves, by order of the Provincial Government. When there is a personal confession from the defendant as prima facie legal evidence, their induction is to take place without necessity of a court verdict. Otherwise, the Prudential Government is to refer the case for a court trial according to the established procedures. Such cases shall also be subject to court trial when a Jewish defendant, due to his unfitness for military service, is subject according to the general determination of the law, and in proportion to the degree of his guilt, to banishment or sentencing to hard labor.

Punishments and Inducements to Ensure Fulfillment of Recruitment Obligation

This decree, passed by Tsar Nicholas I on October 22, 1851, specifies some of the punishments and inducements that proved effective in turning members of the Jewish community against each other.

From: H. Khorobkov, Recruitment of Jews During the Reign of Nicholas I, Yevreiskaya Starina, Volume VI, 1913, p. 239.

If all persons who are fit for service have gone into hiding from a Jewish family from which recruits were to be taken according to the established sequence, recruits shall be taken in the district from the families next in line. However, all runaways shall be presented immediately as recruits, upon being caught or turning themselves in, whenever that might be;

1) If a runaway proves unfit for military service of any kind, he shall be assigned to correctional convict labor gangs of a civilian agency, and afterward, shall not return to his own community but shall be banished to Siberia or some other remote location;

2) Those persons among the Jews who, being next in line for recruitment, but having absented themselves from a recruiting levy in their province, fail to report to their recruiting district before the start of the levy, even if the card has not yet expired, and who fail to submit legal proof that they were unable to report by reason of severe illness, shall be treated in the same manner as above;

3) In Jewish recruiting districts, the heads of households, attorneys of the communities, and in general, people in positions of authority, who have assisted a Jew due for recruitment to avoid military service through the issuing of a pass excusing his absence, likewise in the event that they do not present a fugitive for induction within a week of his capture or appearance, shall themselves be surrendered as recruits without credit. If they are unfit for military service, they shall be assigned to correctional convict labor gangs of a civilian agency for a period of ten to twelve years; and the

Jewish community in which the fugitive has been hidden shall be subject to a monetary penalty of three hundred rubles;

4) Anyone who has caught a Jew who has avoided reporting for recruitment or who has exposed the people harboring such a Jew shall receive a reward of thirty silver rubles from the State Treasury.

Imperial Command to Turn In Vagrants (Piyamnikes)

In the month of July 1853, an Imperial Command encouraged Jews to turn in other Jews not holding valid passports or holding expired passports, whether from their own or other communities, for credit toward their own community's quota.

From: H. Khorobkov, "Recruitment of Jews During the Reign of Nicholas I," Yevreiskaya Starina, Volume VI, 1913, p. 240.

The Jewish communities shall be authorized to detain any Jew who is in hiding from recruitment, or who, in general, is without a passport or has an expired passport. They shall turn him in as a recruit in the place where he is captured, without sending him back to his place of registration. Of such people, those fit for service shall be surrendered as recruits, with credit given to those communities or individuals that have captured the person and presented him to the recruiting office, though he may reside in a community in a different province or district. No credit shall be given for those unfit for service.

This measure shall be enacted for three years as an experiment. At the end of the designated three-year period, the Ministry of Internal Affairs shall be allowed to submit a recommendation concerning the final confirmation of the measure in question, with such revisions and additions as are then deemed necessary.

Receipt of a Chapper
The following receipt was "provided" by a piyamnike, inducted in substitution for a relative of the man who turned him in, releasing his captor from all liability.

From: M. Kagan, "Communications: A Receipt of a Chapper" Yevreiskaya Starina, *Volume III, 1910, p. 427.*

This was given by me, the undersigned, Ovsey Volfovich Petlyuk, a private soldier of the Second Company of the Regiment of Prince Menshikov on temporary leave, to the Jew Movsha Mordukhovich Feldman, a petty bourgeois of Pinsk.

To the effect that I, having been caught by him, Feldman, in 1855, without a written identity card, was given up as a recruit for his (Feldman's) family and have now received full satisfaction in cash from the same Movsha Feldman in return for my entering military service in the name of his family. I declare and hereby attest that I do not have and will not have any claim against Feldman, or any member of his family.

Bibliography

The publications listed in this bibliography can be found in the libraries of the following institutions:

Hebrew University, Jerusalem.

Yeshiva University Mendel Gottesman Library, New York City.

The Y.I.V.O. Institute for Jewish Research, New York City.

University of Florida, Gainesville.

The New York Public Library.

Antin, Mary. *The Promised Land*. Random House, 2001.

Baron, Salo W. *The Russian Jew Under the Tsars and Soviets*. New York, Schocken Books, 1987.

Beylin, S. *Materials and Reports: Tales of Former Cantonist Soldiers, Yevreiskaya Starina*, Volume VII, 1914.

Beylin, S. *Memories of the Last Years of Forced Recruiting, Yevreiskaya Starina*, Volume VII, 1914.

Beylin, S. *Stories About the Cantonists, Yevreiskaya Starina*, Volume I, 1909.

Beylin, S. *Tales of Ex-Cantonists, Yevreiskaya Starina*, Volume VIII, 1915.

Dubnov, Simon. *The History of the Jews in Russia and Poland, Volumes I and II*. Translated from Russian by I. Friedlander. Philadelphia, Jewish Publication Society America, 1918.

Epstein, Baruch Halevi. *Mekor Baruch*. Vilna, Ram Publishers, 1874.

Friedberg, A.S. *Sefer HaShanah* (Yearbook), *Zichronot MiYemei Neurai*, (Remembrances From My Youth), Volume III, Warsaw, 1903.

Galant, I. *Documents From the Era of Nicholas I, Yevreiskaya Starina*, Volume VII, 1914.

Ginsburg, Saul, M. *Historishe Verk, Yiddishe Leiden in Tsarishen Russland* Volume III. (Historical Work, Jewish Martyrdom in Tsarist Russia). New York Saul M. Ginsburg Testimonial Committee, (1915), 1937.

Glitzenstein, Avraham Chanoch (editor and translator). *Sefer HaToldot: Rabbeinu HaTzemach Tzedek* (Our Master and Teacher, The Tzemach Tzedek). Kehot Publishing House, New York, and Kfar Chabad, Israel, 1985.

Herzen, Alexander. *Byloe I Dumy* (My Past Thoughts) Volume I.

Igros Kodesh; The Tzemach Tzedek, (a volume of the *Igros Kodesh* compilation), Kehot Publishers, Brooklyn , New York, 1987, p. 272.

Itzkovich, Israel. *Reminiscences of a Cantonist From Archangelsk. Yevreiskaya Starina,* Volume V, 1912, pp. 54–65.

Kagan, M. *Communications: A Receipt of a Chapper, Yevreiskaya Starina,* Volume III, 1910.

Khorobkov, H. *Recruitment of Jews During the Reign of Nicholas I, Yevreiskaya Starina,* Volume VI, 1913.

Kotik, Yechezkel. *Mayne Zichronos* (My Remembrances). Berlin, Klal Verlag, 1922.

Lebedev, V. *Uchebnyye Vospominaniya,* (School Memoirs), *Russkaya Starina,* Volume VI, 1907.

Levin, Yehudah Leib. *Zichronot Ve-ra'ayanot* (Memoirs and Thoughts). Sefer Ha-yovel huval le-shai Nachum Sokolov. Warsaw, 1904.

Levitats, Isaac. *The Jewish Community in Russia 1844–1917.* New York. Posner and Sons, 1943.

Lewin, Abraham. *Cantonisten: Vegn Der Yiddisher Rekrutshine in Russland in di Tsaytn Fun Tsar Nikolai den Eshten,1827–1855* (Cantonists: About Jewish Recruits in Russia During the Era of Tsar Nicholas I, 1827–1855). Warsaw, Druk Grafia, 1934, (Microfilm, New York Public Library).

Lipschitz, Yaakov HaLevi. *Zichron Yaakov.* Published by Neta HaLevi Lipschitz, son of the author. Israel, 1968.

Merimzon, Chaim. *Razkaz Storago Soldata* (The Story of an Old Soldier), *Yevreiskaya Starina* Vols. V. 1913, 290–301, and 406–422, VI, 1914, 86–95, and 221–232.

Pines, D. *Battles Against the Chappers, Yevreiskaya Starina,* Volume VIII, 1915.

Schneerson, Menachem Mendel (the Tzemach Tzedek). *Derech Mitzvosecha.* Kehot Publishing House, New York, 1996. *Sefer HaSichos* (The Book of Torah Talks). Kehot Publishing House, New York, 1956.

Schwartz, Betzalel and Biletsky, Israel Chaim (editors). *Sefer Kobrin* (The Book of Kobrin), Tel Aviv, 1951.

Sefer HaTamim Periodical, Kehot Publishers, Brooklyn, N.Y. 1972.

Spiegel, Moisy. *From the Notes of a Cantonist, Yevreiskaya Starina,* Volume IV, 1911, 249–259.

Stanislowski, Michael. *Psalms for the Tsar,* New York, Yeshiva University Press, 1988.

Stanislowski, Michael. *Tsar Nicholas and the Jews: The Transformation of Jewish Life in Russia. 1825–1855.* Philadelphia, Jewish Publication Society America, 1983.

Yevreiskaya Starina, Quarterly, Volumes I–VII. St. Petersburg, Jewish Historical Ethnography Society, 1909–1915.

Yosher, Moses M. *The Chafetz Chaim: The Life and Works of Rabbi Yisrael Meir Kagan of Radin.* Translated from English by Charles Wengrov, Art Scroll/Mesorah Publications, New York, 1984

Zeitchik, Chaim. *Moraot Gedolim* (Great Events), Kovno, 1969.

Zunser, Eliakum, *Biographye* (Autobiography), Zunser Jubilee Committee, New York, 1905.

Notes

Chapter 1

[1]Ginsburg, Volume III, p. 107

[2]Dubnov, Volume 1, p.257

[3]Ibid. p. 255

[4]Note:1812 was the year that Napoleon invaded Russia. From Dubnov, Volume II, p. 16.

[5]Dubnov wrote that the term Canton referred to the districts to which the recruits were sent.

[6]Khorobkov, Volume VI p. 242

[7]Baron, p. 29

[8]Dubnov, p. 14

[9]Zamter, *Die Judentaufen im XIX Jahrhundert* (Berlin, 1906), quoted by Khorobkov, p. 243

[10]Records on the number of recruits were not well kept. This figure, based on statistics from the era, is the best available estimate. See Lewin, pp. 159, 160; Stanislowski, p. 24.

[11]Ginsburg, p.33

[12]Lipschitz, Volume III, p. 203

[13]Zunser, p. 14

[14]Dubnov, Volume II. p. 23 includes a Yiddish poem of the time: "When the Ukase came down about Jewish soldiers/ We all dispersed over the lonesome forests./ Over the lonesome forests we all dispersed./ In lonesome pits did we hide ourselves, woe me, woe me."

[15]Over the following years, Tsar Nicholas enacted several laws to eliminate many of the available exemptions. Khorobkov, p. 240.

[16]In 1837, the State Council officially ended the exemption for injury or mutilation and penalized the family of the injured recruit, requiring those who mutilated themselves, along with an additional family member (preferably under age) to join the military. The quota of the community from which the mutilated soldier came would be credited with only one-third of a recruit.

[17]The exemption for married men was enacted in 1835 and resulted in thousands of early marriages. It was fittingly termed the *Behalah* (great confusion). However, many boys who were legally married were nonetheless forced to serve. Often their families lost contact with them. Their departure/disappearance left many married girls in the limbo status of *aguna* (Jewish legal term for an abandoned wife). The number of *agunot* proliferated during this period.

[18]The responsibility of the Kahal was to supervise the moral conduct of the Jewish community and act as a mediator on matters between the Jews and the government. The Kahal employed people in a number of job definitions: leader, trustee, tax collector and assessor, council clerk, and *shtadlan* (an intermediary who acted as the diplomatic spokesman for the community).

[19]Most of the chappers were Jews, but there were also non-Jewish chappers.

[20]See the story "Revolt at Oshitz" in a later chapter of this book.

[21]Ginsburg, p. 29

[22]Igros Kodesh, p. 272. Reference is made to Kahal leaders of Hasidic communities in the regions of Mohlev and Vitebsk who were involved with rescue efforts of Cantonists.

[23]Epstein authored and compiled a commentary on the Pentateuch known as the *Torah Temima*.

[24]Epstein, section II, p. 964

[25]Ibid. p. 965

[26]Levin, p. 355

[27]Zunser, p. 15

[28]This folk poem is quoted in several sources, among them Baron, p. 38 and Levitats, p. 65.

[29]Beylin, Volume VII, p. 459

[30]See Chapter 2 for accounts of abduction of the piyamnikes.

[31]Khorobkov, Volume VI, p. 241

[32]See also Chapter 7 of this book.

[33]Zunser. Purim commemorates the date the Jews' nemesis Haman had planned for their destruction. On that day, instead, the Jews were victorious over their enemies.

Chapter 2

[34]Epstein, p 964

[35]Levin, p. 357

[36]Adapted from Friedberg, Volume III, p. 94

[37]Adapted from Levin, p. 358

[38]Adapted from Ginsburg, p. 31

[39]Adapted from Friedberg, pp. 94–95

[40]Adapted from Friedberg, p.86

[41]Adapted from Pines, p. 398

[42]Israel Salanter, otherwise known as Israel Lipkin (1810–1883) was the chief proponent of the *Mussar* (Moralist) movement.

[43]Adapted from Zeitchik, p. 127

[44]Adapted from Beylin, *Materials and Reports*, p. 461

[45]Adapted from Ginsburg, p. 33

[46]Adapted from Beylin, *Materials and Reports*, p. 461

[47]Ibid. p. 462

[48]Ibid.

Chapter 3

[49]Ginsburg, p. 15

[50]S. Beylin, *Stories About the Cantonists*, p. 117 mentions a mother of a recently recruited Cantonist who heard her son call to her from his company headquarters as she passed it in the street. She stopped to speak with her son and was subsequently arrested and sentenced. Several cases were reported in Siberia of Jewish parents receiving permission to visit their Cantonist children. Within the Pale of Settlement, such contact was generally prohibited.

[51]S. Beylin, *Stories About the Cantonists*, Volume I, p. 120

[52]Lebedev, Volume VI, p. 628

[53]Herzen, Volume I, pp. 314–315

[54]Ginsburg, p. 73

[55]Ibid. p. 88

[56]Beylin, p. 92

[57]Lewin, p. 87

[58]Ginsburg, p. 96
[59]In some cases, torture was the first recourse.
[60]Ginsburg, p. 103
[61]S. Beylin, *Stories About the Cantonists*, Volume I, p. 116
[62]Ginsburg, p. 99
[63]Ibid. p. 114
[64]Ibid. p. 96
[65]Ibid.
[66]Ibid.
[67]S. Beylin, *Stories About the Cantonists*, Volume I, p. 118
[68]Ibid. p. 100
[69]Ibid.
[70]Ibid.
[71]Ibid. p. 101
[72]Ibid.
[73]Ginsburg, p. 64
[74]Ibid. p. 66
[75]Ibid. p. 64
[76]Ibid.
[77]Ibid.
[78]Ibid.
[79]S. Beylin, *Tales of Ex-Cantonists,* Volume VIII, p. 225
[80]Ibid., p. 102
[81]S. Beylin, Materials and Reports, Volume VII, p. 464
[82]Adapted from Kotik, Part One, pp. 177–180

Chapter 4

[83]*Chumash* (Pentateuch); *Rashi* (commentary); *Yavan* (Hebrew for "the Greek." Here reference to a non-Jewish Russian *diadke,* whose role was to usher the youth into the Russian Orthodox faith.); *kittel* (a white ritual garment in which the deceased is dressed for burial); *kapote* (long coat). Poem quoted in Ginsburg, p. 14.
[84]S. Beylin, *Stories About the Cantonists,* Volume I, pp. 115–116
[85]Itzkovich, Volume V, p. 61
[86]Ginsburg, pp. 104–105
[87]Beylin, *Tales of Ex-Cantonists,* Volume VIII, p. 225
[88]Ginsburg, p. 100
[89]Beylin, *Stories About the Cantonists,* Volume I, p. 120
[90]Ginsburg, p. 107
[91]Beylin, *Stories About the Cantonists,* Volume I, p. 119

Chapter 5

[92]Baruch HaLevi Epstein, pp. 966–968
[93]Ginsburg, Volume III, pp. 132–135
[94]Pines, p.396
[95]Friedberg, p. 96, and Schwartz and Biletsky, pp. 33–34
[96]Lewin, p. 184
[97]Rabbi Schneerson, p. 422; Glitzenstein , p. 98. See documents describing the penalties in the appendix of this book
[98]Igros Kodesh; The Tzemach Tzedek, p. 48
[99]Ibid. p. 272
[100]Story authored by Rabbi Avraham Persan, Sefer HaTamim, Second Section, Kehot Publications, 1972, p. 544

[101]Igros Kodesh; The Tzemach Tzedek, Kehot, Brooklyn, NY, 1987, pp. 240, 241

Chapter 6
[102]See Appendix of Documents.
[103]Khorobkov, Volume VI, p. 236
[104]Ginsburg, p. 55
[105]Ginsburg, p 55
[106]Adapted from the account of Asher Kissel of Koritz, recorded in Lewin, p. 156

Chapter 7
[107]Antin, p. 15
[108]Khorobkov, p. 243, quote from V.P.S.Z. Volume 31, No. 30888
[109]Ibid
[110]The era of Syrian Greek rule under Antiochus Epiphanes in the second century B.C.E.
[111]The Holy Ari, Rabbi Isaac Luria (1534-1572) famed kabbalist of Safed
[112]Tzemach Tzedek, *Sefer HaSichos*, pp. 14-15
[113]Lewin, p. 190
[114]Jews cast into a furnace in ancient Babylonia for their beliefs
[115]Adapted from *The Chafetz Chaim: The Life and Works of Rabbi Yisrael Meir Kagan of Radin* by Moses M. Yosher with permission of the copyright holders, ArtScroll/Mesorah Publications, Ltd., pp. 172, 173

Chapter 8
[116]Adapted from Levin, pp. 354-357
[117]Ein Yaakov is a compilation of Midrashic sources from the Talmud

Chapter 9
[118]*Yevreiskaya Starina* Volume V, pp. 54-65
[119]A non-commissioned officer is a military officer appointed from among enlisted personnel.

Chapter 10
[120]In the early seventeenth century the Russian Orthodox Church incorporated more Greek/Byzantine ritual. Some Christians did not accept these reforms and were referred to by the term "Old Believer." The Old Believers (like this unfortunate bishop) were another minority persecuted by Nicholas.

Chapter 11
[121]Some Eastern Catholic churches permit priests to have families if the marriage took place before ordainment.

Chapter 12
[122]Merimzon, *Yevreiskaya Starina* Volumes. V, 1913, pp. 290-301 and 406-422 and VI, 1914, pp. 86-95 and 221-232
[123]See footnote 120
[124]The second line of this psalm is "May God answer you on the day of anguish, may you be made invincible by the name of the God of Jacob."
[125]A liturgical song recited following the conclusion of the Sabbath.
[126]After 1861, promotion to the rank of a noncommissioned officer was also allowed for "unconverted" Jewish soldiers.

Chapter 13

[127]Zunser, pp. 14–19

[128]This holiday recalls ancient celebrations that ushered in the rainy season in the land of Israel.

[129]The Russian oven, the top of which could be used as a bed, was a standard household fixture.

[130]A series of hymns and prayers recited in praise of God on certain holidays and particularly joyous occasions.

Chapter 14

[131]*Okhotnik* (literally, "hunter;" the same word is used for "volunteer") was a pejorative term used by the Jews in Lithuania for a dissolute person, rowdy person, glutton, and drunkard.